Ho Chi Minh City 2018

Table of Contents

Introduction

Welcome to Ho Chi Minh City! Also known as Saigon (Ho Chi Minh City became the official name in 1976), this booming yet still-developing metropolis is a unique vortex of ceaseless street noise, electric colors, tempting scents and aromas, mysterious cuisine, inviting smiles, and a dizzying current of clamorous excitement that extends hurriedly and endlessly in every direction.

The city is regularly used as a gateway to the many beautiful sights of the countryside, including rivers, mountains, and the spectacular shores and islands of Vietnam. Yet, it is itself a city worthy of getting to know intimately. It is like no other in the world, and its many previously forbidden mysteries can quickly be unlocked, accessed, and enjoyed with some easy reading. Spend some time here in the maelstrom of this southern Vietnamese metropolis, and your life and world perspective will undoubtedly be touched, if not significantly changed.

Downtown along the Saigon River

The sprawling maze of boulevards, backstreets, and alleyways in this corner of Indochina connects a city that is psychologically encumbered by a brutal past of bombs, seemingly endless war, and sadly, mass death. Yet, the cacophony of the night revelry appears to indicate little memory of Vietnam's destructive and tragic history. After all, 85 percent of the current population was born after the fall of Saigon in 1975. Only trace vestiges in the citizens' collective memory of that horrific era remain.

Architectural relics are evident (but fading away at an alarming rate) of its French colonial past, where romantic villas are graced with the lengthy, bright green leaves of banana trees, covering otherwise open-air dining rooms in a unique splendor of *La Belle Époque*-meets-the-Southeast-Asian-jungle. Yet, popping through the stifling heat are the gleaming skyscrapers of a modern, thriving Asian city, illuminating the night with the entire spectrum of color. Sadly, some of the city's charm is being bulldozed to make room for these skyscrapers along with the construction of a spreading network of super highways. But if you hurry, you can witness the enthralling affirmations of the past converging with the developing present before many of them disappear into the annals of history.

Old stalwart hotels like the Rex and the Caravelle stand side-by-side with the contemporary Sheraton, Le Meridien, and Park Hyatt luxury varieties, all with rooms that are generally in plentiful supply. Modern rooftop clubs compete with the classic 1920s jazz-style nightlife, and of course rock-n-roll can be found in every quarter. A sea of mobile phones glow and buzz among the flowered storefronts and traditional eateries, and black, cool sunglasses adorn the youth. A cultural transformation is clearly underway.

Swarms of motorbikes hum and purr in parades of directional randomness. These two-wheel machines move families, sometimes five to a cycle, in the choking evening heat while taxis struggle their way through the horn-honking din. One can stare hopelessly at street scenes that seem to be devoid of any sort of traffic plan. Tourists attempt to cross the chaotic streets, quickly and frightfully learning how to navigate the endless river of motorbikes and other vehicles.

Beautiful young women grace the streets in traditional, famously colorful *ao dai* dresses. Some are fronting restaurants and beckoning customers with welcoming smiles that convey the warmth of the tropics. The younger girls in the traditional white dresses reserved for school days are cheerfully at play after their homework is complete. Those a few years older with several years of city-life experience typically don more colorful apparel and are far more business-oriented with countenances of ambition.

Elder women wear conical hats with shoulder poles. They carry their carefully balanced cargo to-and-fro as the bustle of street life spills every which way. Men of all ages jackhammer streets, shovel mounds of dirt, and move merchandise in and out of storefronts. Their cargo of coconuts, jackfruit, mangoes, vibrantly hued flowers, the famous *banh mi* sandwiches, fresh green summer rolls, and creative souvenirs gets shuffled around and peddled in the streets with hurried purpose.

Troops of variedly aged Buddhist monks solemnly march by, perhaps headed to the many pagodas within the city, or just out for some evening meditation. They pass young local lovers strolling hand-in-hand, smiling and giggling deep into the night. The scent of a suspenseful and gripping Graham Greene novel is ubiquitously in the air.

Charcoal barbecues sizzle with shellfish, river fish, chicken, red meat, and vegetables over hot coals that glow, crackle and dance with flame throughout nearly every block. Hordes of customers swill Saigon Beer and toast one another into the night, often ritualistically challenging each other to finish "100 percent" of a can of beer to demonstrate virility. Steaming pots of flavorful *pho*, the national dish of Vietnam, and other spicy noodle soups simmer in the night, releasing their herbal fragrances to the masses. Tiny, fully peeled local bananas char over open fires, waiting to be smothered in warm, thick coconut sauce. Little street food stalls compete with beautiful villa courtyards for dining customers, often with equally compelling fare, such as fresh water elephant fish from the Mekong River. Diners cheerfully pluck the dishes with chopsticks and dip the goodness into a swirling combination of salt, lime juice, black pepper, and locally grown red bird's eye chili peppers. Traditional, ancient cuisine shares the sidewalk with modern culinary invention. All of it tickles your nose.

And yes, there is a seedy side to the city, with back alley massage parlors, tourist rip-offs, bait-and-switch scams, purse-snatching cyclists, and business men and women not necessarily working in the best interests of their fellow citizens, much less tourists. They prowl the streets, where hard currency is the only real currency. These, however, are only slight distractions from the goodness you are about to experience, as most Vietnamese people you will encounter are gentle, honest, fragile, friendly, artistic, and emotionally complex. Just be aware, as with anywhere, some shameful shiftiness exists. Vigilance will help to avoid it.

Welcome to Saigon, or rather Ho Chi Minh City, its relatively recent, politically inspired name. This book will provide you a foundation of knowledge to help maximize the enjoyment of your visit in this aging city on the brink of modernity. There is much to learn about this mysterious corner of the world. First-time visitors will find many experiences to discover and enjoy. Those that are returning will undoubtedly discover much that is new and captivating. You are in for quite a ride. Hang on, be safe, and have fun!

Ho Chi Minh City at night (Thoai/Shutterstock.com)

About this Book

To truly navigate and discover the depths of wonder Ho Chi Minh City has to offer, some research prior to a visit will be immeasurably helpful. To assist in planning, the author has provided detailed content for a comprehensive set of subjects about Ho Chi Minh City. This collection of knowledge and experience should abundantly prepare the traveler for his or her stay. It will also serve as a detailed trip reference guide, helping to achieve the maximum memorable experience intricately tailored to one's interests.

This thorough travel volume explores the city's troubled history, unique culture, fascinating people, unforgettable cuisine (national and regional), top attractions, and other items of significant tourist and business traveler interest. Features include profiles of a hand-selected set of restaurants (Vietnamese and international), a nightlife and entertainment review, recommended hotels for all budgets, a detailed walking tour of the heart of the city, transportation options, local tour offerings, current economic information, an introduction to the language, and a guide to selected nearby destinations. Several up-to-date maps for hotels, restaurants, nightlife, cafes, and a walking tour will aid in the experience such as these:

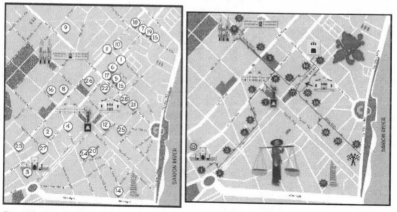

Sample maps found within the book: restaurant map and a walking tour map

There is also a "best of" collection of activities, local dishes to try, profiles of the city's top coffee shops, tours of all kinds, landmarks, major sights, temple information, and historical descriptions gathered after the author's ten visits to the city over a period of twelve years, including multiple-month stays, and made available to you for the purposes of enhancing your experience. These summaries will make your visit much more intense, action-packed, comprehensive, enjoyable, and rewarding.

Additionally, this book takes an especially close look at the uniquely sensational and celebrated cuisine of not only Ho Chi Minh City, but also all of Vietnam, as traditional dishes and dedicated restaurants from all over the country can be found within the city, the culinary capital of Vietnam. This includes some helpful graphics such as the following:

Sample cuisine highlights

Also included is a well-researched historical summary and timeline of the city from its Khmer, Cham, and Chinese-influenced beginnings, to the French colonial age and its effects, the Japanese occupation during the Second World War, the Cold War period leading up to and including the Vietnam War, the communist era, the city's modern challenges, and a forward-looking path among other Asian cities.

There is specific pragmatic information for travelers for pre-trip planning and of use while visiting the energetic and enigmatic city as well. This includes obtaining a visa in advance of a trip, currency information, expected weather, health considerations, and technological communication recommendations such as available mobile device services and alternatives.

This primer on the city is ideal for either a quick trip or an extended stay. Reading this book will provide you with an enriching foundation of insight to maximize the enjoyment of your visit. There is much to learn about this exotic corner of the world.

Location

Vietnam is in Southeast Asia and is the easternmost country of Indochina, the continental land mass lying east of India and south of China. Vietnam is to the east of shared borders with Cambodia and Laos and to the south of a shared border with China. Its coastline sits primarily on the South China Sea. A portion of the southernmost coast is on the Gulf of Thailand as is the Vietnamese island of Phu Quoc. Parts of northern Vietnam have coastline on the Gulf of Tonkin. The seven thousand islands of the Philippines are directly to the east of Vietnam across the South China Sea. If you travel south from the southern tip of Vietnam, you will reach Singapore on the southern end of the Malaysian peninsula. Vietnam is located entirely between the Tropic of Cancer and the Equator, making it a tropical nation.

Ho Chi Minh City, the country's largest city, is in the far southern segment of Vietnam. Hanoi, the nation's capital, is seven hundred miles away in the far north of the country. The Saigon River snakes its way through Ho Chi Minh City before it empties into the South China Sea not far from the port city of Vung Tau. The Mekong River, entering Vietnam by way of Cambodia, is a two-hour drive to the south in the heart of the Mekong Delta region, where its distributaries split off and empty into the South China Sea. The latitude of Ho Chi Minh City is similar to that of San José, Costa Rica and Caracas, Venezuela in the Americas.

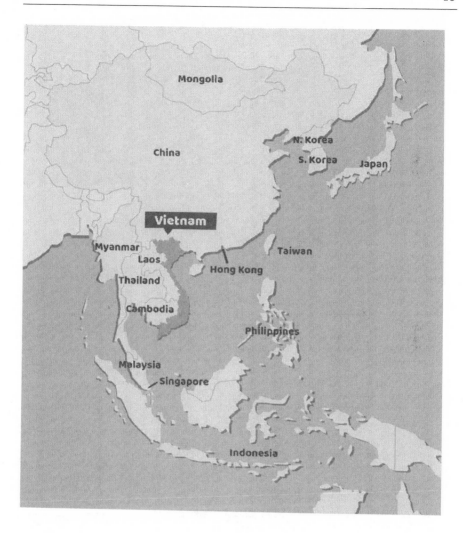

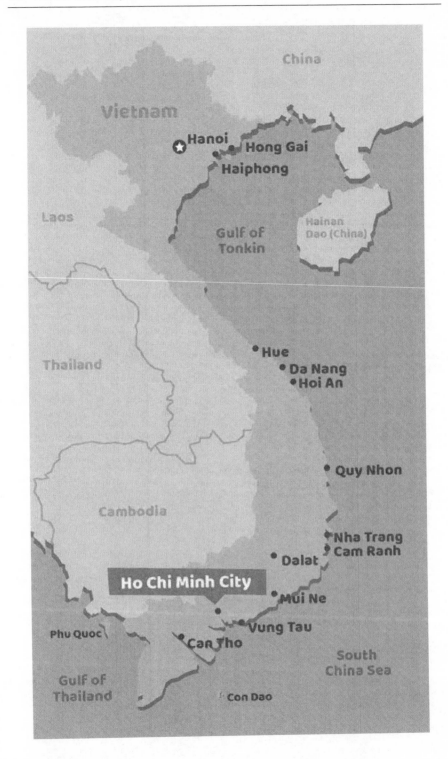

Planning Ahead

When to Go

Ho Chi Minh City has a tropical climate and is hot all year long. Fortunately, the city doesn't suffer from monsoons and floods to the extent northern and central Vietnam do.

The city has two seasons: the dry season and the wet season. The dry season lasts from December to April. Although this period experiences the hottest temperatures, there is less humidity. This provides for a more comfortable climate than other times of year.

March, April, and May have the highest average temperatures. This period occasionally culminates in triple-digit territory in April at the end of the dry season. High temperatures can average 95 degrees Fahrenheit (35 degrees Celsius) during this time. The three-month span of December through February represents a milder weather interval, but still maintains appreciable amounts of daytime heat. During this time, the temperatures reside in the upper 80s and lower 90s (30-34 degrees Celsius). If you have flexibility, this is probably the best time to visit.

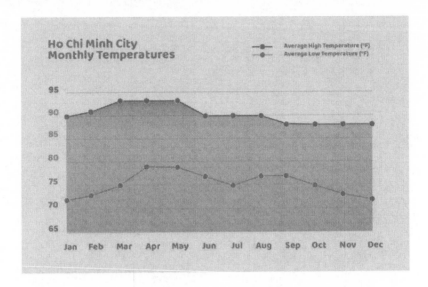

The wet season, lasting from May to November, often consists of brief afternoon rains and occasional thunderstorms. This is monsoon season, with periods of uncomfortably high humidity paired with tropical weather. If you have spent any time in summer in the southeastern United States in places like Louisiana, Georgia, South Carolina, or Florida, you have likely experienced similar, though perhaps not as drastic, hot, humid, and potentially stormy weather.

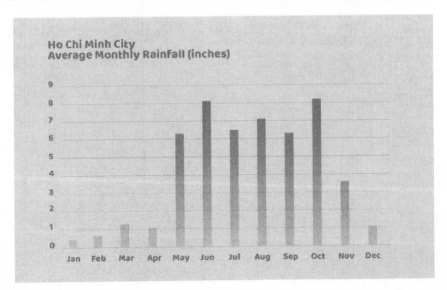

You may hear a Vietnamese person refer to a cloudy, overcast day as a "beautiful day." This is because the clouds can provide a welcome break from the seemingly endless days of scorching heat.

Whatever time you go, there will not be a tremendous amount of temperature variability. It will be hot, and you are going to sweat, perhaps profusely at times. Be prepared for extensive and unremitting heat. Dress appropriately, and generously apply sunscreen multiple times per day to protect yourself from the intense sun. Always carry (or have money with you to purchase) plenty of bottled water, regardless of the time of year you visit.

For further and current weather information, consult the following websites:

Vietnam National Weather Center:
www.nchmf.gov.vn/Web/en-US/43/Default.aspx

World Meteorological Association:
worldweather.wmo.int/en/city.html?cityId=309

Itineraries

Since trip lengths will vary, here are some recommended traveler's priorities. If your visit is three days or fewer, these suggestions will help maximize your time and experience. If you are staying longer, these can provide for a great starting point.

One day: Start early and spend the morning doing the _Walking Tour_ described in this book. It will be a grand, comprehensive introduction and cover many of the major sights in Ho Chi Minh City, including Ben Thanh Market, the venerable Dong Khoi Street, and several famous examples of French colonial architecture. A fun choice for lunch is Nha Hang Ngon on Pasteur Street for a wide variety of traditional Vietnamese food to see and enjoy (see _Where to Eat_).

In the afternoon, step into the past at nearby Reunification Palace, the former Republic of South Vietnam headquarters, preserved as it was in the last days of South Vietnam's existence in 1975 before it fell to the communists. In the evening, try one of the beautiful upscale Vietnamese restaurants noted in the *Where to Eat* section. Then finish off the night in one of the many rooftop bars listed in the *Nightlife* section and enjoy spectacular views of the illuminated cityscape.

Two days: Follow the one-day itinerary on the first day. On the second morning, enjoy one or more of the many coffee shops listed in the *Coffee Shop Culture* section. Finish the morning by visiting one of the temples listed under *Major Sights*. The Jade Emperor Pagoda is a great choice. Have lunch at any of the *pho* or *bun bo Hue* restaurants listed in the *Where to Eat* section to immerse yourself in Ho Chi Minh City's unique and delicious soup culture.

In the afternoon, beat the heat with a relaxing, long, invigorating massage at one of the establishments listed in the *Massage* section of this book. For the evening (including dinner), book one of the various cuisine-oriented motorbike tours listed in the *Tours and Activities* section (you will be well-rested from your massage). If you still have energy, finish off the night swilling a cold beer or three on electric, never-dull Bui Vien Street.

Three days: After following the two-day itinerary, the third day would be fitting for a scenic trip down the Mekong River utilizing one of the tourist methods listed in the *Tours and Activities* section. Also see *Side Trips* for more information about the Mekong Delta region and tour options. If you prefer to stay within the city instead, the *Hoa Tuc Cooking Class* is an exceptional way to experience the local cuisine in the morning and includes lunch as part of the curriculum. In the latter case, either the *Fine Arts Museum* or the *War Remnants Museum* would be a scholarly way to spend at least part of the afternoon.

For dinner, try one of the many beautiful French restaurants in town and imagine returning to the era of colonial Saigon. Finish off the evening at one of the live music establishments listed in the *Nightlife* section.

Obtaining a Visa and Consular Information

To enter Vietnam from most countries, you will need a visa. For the majority of Western travelers, this means a tourist visa. Other types of visas or entry documents can be obtained in place of a tourist visa depending on the nature of your visit. In this book we will concentrate on the tourist visa process for US citizens (although relevant information is in this section for other nationalities). As long as you give yourself plenty of time (preferably a month if you already have a passport), it is a straightforward process.

To obtain a tourist visa, you will need to have a valid passport. The passport will need to have at least six months of validity remaining beyond your arrival date.

If you do not have a passport, you will need to get one prior to obtaining your tourist visa. You should allow a month or two if you need to acquire a passport in addition to the processing time subsequently required for the tourist visa. You can pay a higher fee to expedite the process of obtaining a passport.

If this is your first time obtaining a passport, you will need to appear in person at a passport agency. If you need to renew one and meet certain conditions, you can do so by mail. For more information about obtaining a US passport, visit the US Department of State's website at **travel.state.gov**. For other countries, consult your own state department websites for passport-related information.

To obtain a standard tourist visa before your departure to Vietnam, apply either in person or via mail with the Vietnamese Embassy in Washington, DC. You must first complete the application online. You will then need to submit your passport and the appropriate fees. For complete instructions in the US, visit the Vietnamese Embassy website at **vietnamembassy-usa.org**.

You can also apply in person or via regular mail at the three Vietnamese consulates in the US in San Francisco, New York City, or Houston. In Canada, apply at the embassy in Ottawa or at the consulate in Vancouver. In the United Kingdom, apply at the embassy in London. In Australia, apply at the embassy in Canberra, or at the consulates in Perth or Sydney. In New Zealand, apply at the embassy in Wellington.

A tourist visa application form and current visa-related information can be obtained at the following website: **visa.mofa.gov.vn/Homepage.aspx**.

You can apply for your tourist visa as early as six months prior to your trip. Be sure your passport has empty pages available for the tourist visa. In years past in the US, if you were running low on empty passport pages, you could send in your passport to have extra pages added. Now, however, you *must* apply with the US Department of State for an entirely new passport. If you travel internationally frequently, order your new passport with fifty-two pages rather than the standard twenty-eight pages at no additional cost.

If you are pressed for time or your trip is very soon, it is possible to receive a visa-on-arrival in Vietnam if you have an approval letter and are arriving via airplane at the Ho Chi Minh City airport. For more information about a visa-on-arrival, you can visit third-party websites such as **www.myvietnamvisa.com**, **www.vietnam-visa.org**, or **www.visa4vietnam.com**. There may be restrictions on reasons for receiving the required approval letter.

To avoid unnecessary complications, obtain your tourist visa well before your trip. Sadly, people have been sent home from the airports in Vietnam for not having the proper entry authorization.

US citizens can also sign up for the Smart Traveler Enrollment Program (STEP) at the US Department of State website to receive via email the latest travel updates, alerts, and warnings for the countries you select. This includes any emergency notifications during your trip.

Airline Information

Air travel to Ho Chi Minh City originating from the United States usually involves western connections through Hong Kong, Tokyo, Bangkok, Seoul, Taipei, or Singapore. Those in the eastern US have some additional options for eastward connections, such as via Europe or the Middle East, although westward connections are usually still quicker. United Airlines and Delta Airlines are the only US carriers to fly into Ho Chi Minh City, but they do not fly directly from airports within the United States. Other US airlines such as American Airlines offer Ho Chi Minh City as a destination via codeshare routes, meaning you fly another airline for at least some of the trip.

The following are major airlines that at the time of this writing provide commercial service into Ho Chi Minh City: United Airlines, Delta, Air France, Japan Airlines, Korean Air, Singapore Airlines, Emirates, Vietnam Airlines, Cathay Pacific, EVA Air, China Airlines, Air China, China Eastern Airlines, China Southern Airlines, Malaysia Airlines, Turkish Airlines, Qatar Airlines, Etihad Airways, Air New Zealand, and Aeroflot. Additional major international carriers such as Lufthansa, Qantas, British Airways, and several others offer service to Ho Chi Minh City via codeshare.

Vietnam Airlines provides service into Ho Chi Minh City from several non-Asian cities such as Frankfurt, Paris, London, Sydney, and Melbourne. It serves Ho Chi Minh City from several other Asian cities, including Bangkok, Singapore, Jakarta, Kuala Lumpur, Siem Reap, Phnom Penh, Hong Kong, Shanghai, Beijing, Guangzhou, Yangon, Tokyo, Taipei, Osaka, and a few others.

Within Vietnam, you can fly Vietnam Airlines to Ho Chi Minh City from Hanoi, Danang, Nha Trang, Dalat, Hue, Phu Quoc, Con Dao, and a handful of other smaller airports.

Fares vary widely on international flights to Ho Chi Minh City. Prices can rise significantly around busy Western holidays such as Christmas and New Year's as Vietnamese-Americans and Vietnamese from other parts of the world often travel en masse to Vietnam during this period. Also, around the Vietnamese Tet (Lunar New Year) holiday, travel in and out of Ho Chi Minh City can be expensive (and check-in lines can be long). Generally, fares rise in the summertime as well. They can also jump significantly from day to day. Check often and try several different combinations of arrival and departure days for the best fares if you have the travel flexibility to do so.

For travel deals, current fares, and ticket purchases, check airline aggregation websites such as Google Flights, Kayak, Expedia, Orbitz, and others that offer online price comparison tools. It is also beneficial to go to individual airline sites as fares can be substantially different from what the fare aggregation sites are showing.

If you intend to travel within Vietnam or nearby countries, it is usually cheaper to book with Vietnam Airlines or other regional carriers directly from their websites, as the international airline travel aggregation websites often add a premium (sometimes a substantial one) when purchasing airfare through them. In Ho Chi Minh City, there are several Vietnam Airlines ticket offices you can visit, including a large, comfortable ticket office in the Union Square shopping complex (171 Dong Khoi Street, District 1) where you can discuss flight options and often secure the best fares, even last minute or near to your travel date.

Flight information can change; especially as new airlines add service to Ho Chi Minh City. Inevitably, certain airlines may also choose to drop service for business reasons. Connection cities may be altered and airlines merge. Flight arrangements, probably more than any other component of your trip, deserve a substantial amount of online research to obtain current, accurate, and useful information prior to traveling.

Mobile Devices

To have a local phone number while in Ho Chi Minh City, bring an unlocked mobile phone or similar device on your trip. This will enable you to use a "sim" card that will provide you with a local number. You can then make inexpensive calls and use a local data plan. This will be helpful in making reservations at restaurants and using car services like Uber. It will make it easier for locals to reach you if necessary. Also, in the endless maze of streets and alleys that is Ho Chi Minh City, a smart device with GPS is a must.

Sim cards are inexpensive and readily available, including at the airport, the post office, and several mobile service company locations throughout Ho Chi Minh City. Many of the youth prefer Vinaphone and Mobifone for their fast data speeds. You can buy a Mobifone sim card at the Mobifone store on Nguyen Du Street between Dong Khoi and Hai Ba Trung. A Vinaphone sim card can be purchased at the Vinaphone store on the same block.

If you are traveling to rural sections of Vietnam, consider choosing a sim card and network access from state-owned Viettel, the largest mobile operator in Vietnam. Viettel has a broader reach into more remote areas of the country.

If you use your own cell phone from home with an international data plan, phone call and data charges can be exorbitant. These charges can provide for a painful moment when the bill arrives after your trip. Knowing that a local sim card with data and a reasonable block of calling minutes (such as a 100-minute package) will likely cost you between $10 and $15, going local is the obvious (not to mention "cool") choice.

Most carriers in the US and other countries these days do allow for plans with unlocked phones, enabling you to use your own phone with a local sim card. If yours does not, you might be able to borrow one from your carrier's store where you live or from a friend. If that is not possible, you can obtain an unlocked mobile phone from online retailers such as Amazon or eBay, or at many non-carrier mobile phone stores (mainly used mobile phone stores) in your own city. Bare bones devices and phones that are a version or two behind will be more than sufficient.

Google's Project Fi service, which uses Wi-Fi networks to provide calling capabilities utilizing voice-over-ip (VoIP) techniques, has service in Ho Chi Minh City. This means you can use your home Project Fi data plan with your current mobile device without additional cost and make inexpensive local calls without the use of a local sim card. You will have the same phone number as you do at home.

The coverage of Project Fi will likely only grow and improve over time. At present, it is only available on a select number of devices. The drawback is that it is more difficult for locals to call an international number.

Internet

High-speed Internet is widely available throughout Ho Chi Minh City. The newer hotels have excellent Internet speed and service, and most of the smaller, older hotels provide at least adequate service. Some of the inexpensive hotels will have slower access speeds.

Many restaurants, bars, and public locations also offer free Wi-Fi. In restaurants, for example, simply ask your server for the password.

You should be pleasantly surprised with the Internet infrastructure and access speeds within Vietnam, especially as compared with other developing countries.

Money and Currency

The currency of Vietnam is the Vietnamese *dong* (pronounced "dalm"). In its present form, it has been the currency of Vietnam since 1978. At the time of this writing, one US dollar equals approximately 23,000 Vietnamese dong (abbreviated VND). Unfortunately, this can make the math quite tricky from time to time when calculating the cost of an item in a shop or marketplace based on equal value in another currency. A good rule of thumb to help you do the math when thinking about prices is that one million dong is approximately fifty US dollars (closer to $44). If someone mentions something costs five million dong, with some simple math you know in your head it is in the ballpark of $250.

1 million VND = approximately $50 USD (but closer to $44)
2 million VND = approximately $100 USD (but closer to $88)

To retrieve current exchange rates for Vietnamese currency against several other foreign currencies, including the US dollar, visit Vietcom Bank's currency rate website:

www.vietcombank.com.vn/exchangerates

Bringing Cash

It is a good idea to bring at least a few hundred dollars or the equivalent foreign currency on your trip as a backup to ATM cards. Unlike many cities in Europe, you can receive decent exchange rates in Ho Chi Minh City at the various money changing vendors around town. Be sure to check the rates, especially if there are "no commission" signs, as vendors often make up the lack of a commission with a poor exchange rate. It is also wise to ask up front how much in Vietnamese currency you will receive in the exchange *before* you hand over any money to avoid any misunderstandings. Be wary of some commercial money changers, especially international chains that show currency conversion in odd multiples such as sixty or six hundred. One need only wonder why they would promote confusing exchange rate math unless their intentions were to indeed confuse you and score large commissions in the process.

If you bring US dollars or the equivalent, convert it into the local currency first rather than attempting to spend it. Some restaurants and merchants will accept US dollars or euros for example, but you will get a less-than-stellar exchange rate for any transaction.

If you do choose to convert money into Vietnamese dong prior to your trip, you also will not get a great exchange rate. Be aware that the Vietnamese inspect currency closely when any kind of cash transaction occurs. If a currency note is torn, wrinkled, or written on in any way, currency exchangers will not accept it. Neither will banks, merchants, or anyone else. This could render currency bills worthless if they are in anything less than perfect condition. You should inspect any currency notes you receive while in Vietnam as well, as someone might attempt to pawn off money in an unacceptable condition on an unsuspecting tourist.

With few exceptions, it is best to plan to use ATM cards and wait until you get to Vietnam to exchange your own currency into Vietnamese dong. Still, it can't hurt to have some local currency on arrival at the airport to pay your taxi fare to your hotel, along with some reserve cash. Also, be sure to check that your ATM card works in Ho Chi Minh City before you travel.

Credit and Debit Cards

These days, credit cards are accepted at hotels, restaurants, and within many of the various shopping establishments in Ho Chi Minh City (although most market stalls and street food vendors only take cash). Bring at least one credit card, and two or more if possible.

Many credit cards are available that do not charge international fees when using them. Be sure to understand what fees your bank charges while abroad. If necessary, shop around for a no-international-transaction-fee credit card or discuss obtaining this option with your bank for your current credit card(s). Otherwise, transaction fees can be 3 percent or more. Be sure and notify your bank that you will be traveling to Vietnam to help avoid the chance that they might lock your card for security reasons once transactions in Vietnam begin to occur.

It is easy to get Vietnamese dong out of ATMs with a US or international debit card, but again be mindful of your bank's ATM charges and conversion rates. These fees can add up quickly. In some cases, they can be outrageously high and tantamount to theft. Where possible, check out the partner networks and "global alliance partners" of your personal bank as using your own bank or partner ATMs can help reduce fees. Within certain partner networks, some ATMs charge fees while others do not.

Citibank, headquartered in New York City, HSBC, headquartered in London, and ANZ, headquartered in Melbourne, all have significant presence in Ho Chi Minh City. Having accounts at any of these banks may help avoid ATM fees and make any necessary banking easier. Debit cards of other international banks tend to work fine in Ho Chi Minh City and other cities and towns. If possible, bring some cash and multiple cards in case there is some difficulty with any given card or banking network once you arrive. This can help avoid any unpleasant financial experiences.

Booking Rooms in Advance

While hotels are described in detail later in this book, here are a few tips for handling your accommodations when planning a trip to Ho Chi Minh City. First, as always, book as early as possible. Some dates are more difficult than others for finding a preferred, comfortable, and convenient place to stay.

Much of your time as a tourist will likely be spent in and around District 1. It is recommended to stay within this district, or very close to it. This will minimize time traveling around a city with exceptionally high temperatures.

In general, and at least for now, accommodations are less expensive in Ho Chi Minh City versus other world cities. Depending on your budget, there is a wide range of accommodation possibilities. You can spend $150 to $250+ USD per night in some of the more posh, luxurious hotels such as the Park Hyatt or the Sheraton and have every comfort at your disposal. There are also several classy and sophisticated mid-range hotels that list around $100 USD per night, including the Grand, the Prince Hotel (formerly the Duxton), and the three Liberty-brand hotels. Attractive for the budget-conscious are the various "mini-hotels" that are charmingly local in character and can range in price from $35 to $75 USD per night. Despite the lower prices, these smaller hotels are normally quite comfortable, are in favorable locations, and provide standard amenities such as Wi-Fi. They almost always provide a traditional Vietnamese breakfast, often with Western items.

There are many "serviced apartments" which are not too expensive and could be ideal for longer stays, especially if you are looking for amenities such as a kitchen, living room, and more on-site facilities, or if you are traveling as a family. These are worth considering.

When searching, visit the websites of individual hotels as well as the hotel aggregation sites such as Priceline, Hotwire, Expedia, and the like. Remember that many of the hotels in the city don't have relationships with these services, especially the mini-hotels. It can be advantageous to call hotels directly as you might nab a better deal and possibly even negotiate a discount. You might obtain a better rate agreeing to pay cash, while also avoiding international credit card conversion fees. Remember, if you choose this route and pay for your hotel in cash up front upon arrival, you will want to be sure to be given a receipt to avoid any difficulty or misunderstanding about the bill upon checkout.

Be sure and call to confirm your hotel a few days prior to your arrival. Sometimes mistakes and miscommunication can happen. You don't want to find yourself without a room late at night upon arrival, exhausted after a long-haul flight.

Keeping Healthy

Like with most things, it's not possible to be 100 percent free of health risk while traveling in Asia. However, you can significantly reduce the chance of minor or significant illness by employing some commonsense tips during your stay. Even careful travelers can procure stomach ailments requiring frequent bathroom visits while in Ho Chi Minh City. Being prepared to treat such an eventuality is useful. It would be wise to bring stomach malady medication with you on your trip. Recognize sanitation requirements are not as strict in Vietnam as they are in most Western cities. There are continuing efforts, however, geared towards public health in Ho Chi Minh City that should continue to improve over time. In the meantime, being careful and practicing proper hygiene is an excellent idea.

Avoid tap water as it can be contaminated with bacteria that has seeped into porous underground pipes. Use bottled water or filtered water when possible, including when brushing your teeth. Be careful not to orally consume any water while taking a shower. Salad and vegetables are sometimes risky as they may have been washed with contaminated water if a restaurant is not practicing meticulous hygiene, and eating them could make you ill. Fruits with inedible skins that can be peeled are always a great choice. Inspect eating utensils, dishes, and bowls and wipe them down with a napkin if there happens to be any water present. Be aware that some street vendors fill up discarded, empty water bottles with tap water. Be judicious as to where you purchase your bottled water. Commercial locations are better.

Coffee and tea is made from boiled water, which kills bacteria, and therefore is likely fine. Most restaurants purchase their ice from filtered sources, so it is usually ok. Avoid ice chips from large blocks of ice, including crushed ice.

When considering restaurants, observe the general cleanliness of the place, including the food preparation areas. If you see anything that looks suspect, try somewhere else. Understand that busier places with a higher volume of customers are more likely to be serving fresh foods. Ensure that all consumed meats are 100 percent cooked. In the finer restaurants, medium-rare steaks should be ok, but it is wise to adhere to an abundance of caution.

As a major urban area, and with all the gasoline-powered motorbikes buzzing about, quality of air is an issue in Ho Chi Minh City. If you are operating or on the back of a motorized bike frequently during your visit, consider buying a mask to avoid breathing the unhealthy elements present in the air. These are available inexpensively from many street vendors. Be sure to wear a helmet as accidents often happen, and head injuries are no fun.

As you will quickly learn, the sun is quite intense in Ho Chi Minh City and sunscreen is a must. Sunglasses can help prevent burning eyes. Use insect spray, especially in the countryside, as dengue fever and malaria are potential risks.

You may encounter the occasional stray animal in Ho Chi Minh City. Avoid them, as they may have rabies or other diseases, even if they appear cute and cuddly.

If ill or injured, here are three medical centers to consider:

Columbia Asia Saigon Medical Center (District 1)
08 Alexandre de Rhodes
(+84 8 3823 8888)
www.columbiaasia.com/saigon

FV Hospital Saigon (District 7)
Phu My Hung
6 Nguyen Luong Bang
(+84 8 5411 3333)
www.fvhospital.com/en

FV Saigon Clinic (District 1)
Third floor, Bitexco Financial Tower
2 Hai Trieu Street
(+84 8 6290 6167)
www.fvhospital.com/en

For more detailed information on keeping healthy while in Ho Chi Minh City, including current vaccination suggestions and alternatives as to where to receive medical care if necessary, visit the US Center for Disease Control (CDC) website at **wwwnc.cdc.gov/travel/destinations/traveler/none/vietnam**.

Additional Considerations

As with any destination, you may want to explore travel insurance. It can be a wise investment, especially if you are pre-paying for any kind of organized tours. An ideal policy will cover lost baggage, medical costs, and other trip or tour cancellation costs. A suggested website to explore different policies is at **www.insuremytrip.com**.

Be sure to take photocopies or digital scans of your passport and visa and keep them with you. Keep the digital versions in an accessible, secure email account or stored on a mobile device or laptop, otherwise it will be difficult to replace your passport should it be lost or stolen.

Vietnam's electrical system, like Europe, is 220 volts. This is different from the 110-volt system in North America. If traveling from the US or Canada, you will need to bring electrical adapters (and possibly converters for older devices) for your appliances, chargers, and other electronics.

A Brief History

Birth of a City

The land that is today's Ho Chi Minh City, now Vietnam's largest metropolitan area, was originally heavily forested swampland. Before the Vietnamese arrived from the north to lay permanent claim in the 17th century, it had been settled by the Khmer people of the medieval Angkor civilization, whose descendants today are the largest ethnic group in Cambodia. Before that, fragments of the ancient kingdom of Champa, a Hindu-influenced civilization that reached its zenith a thousand years ago throughout central Vietnam, existed here.

During the Khmer period, the village was called Prey Nokor, one of several different names in the city's history. The Khmer named it as such after they had invaded and defeated the Champa people of the region in the 12th century. The Khmer Empire was quite large at the time, also encompassing much of modern Cambodia, Thailand, and Malaysia.

Cham ruins in southern Vietnam (Tran Nuoc Dung/Shutterstock.com)

This village became an important seaport for the Khmer thanks to the waterway known today as the Saigon River, a major water vessel route that flows into the South China Sea. The Saigon River also connects to the Dong Nai River heading northward and enables easy access to the Mekong River because of the proximity of the Saigon and Mekong river mouths on the coast. This network of rivers provided the Khmer with trading ability throughout much of Southeast Asia at the time. Commerce consisted primarily of buffalo-driven rice farming, which enabled the local culture to flourish throughout the region.

The original Vietnamese civilization emerged in what is today northern Vietnam. Part of China's Han dynasty over two thousand years ago, it had become a separate region from China with its own language and culture. For nearly a thousand years after inclusion in the Han dynasty, the Vietnamese still lived under Chinese rule until independence was achieved in 938 A.D.

In the early 17th century, nobles of the Nguyen dynasty (pronounced "win") ruling from the then Vietnamese capital of Hue (pronounced "hway") in central Vietnam, began desiring expansion. Since the juggernaut China existed to the north, these nobles looked southward and began establishing camps in and around what would become Ho Chi Minh City, displacing the Khmer people who were living there at the time.

In 1698, the Nguyen nobles in Hue officially annexed a large segment of territory that included Prey Nokor. This incursion marks the official beginning of Saigon, Ho Chi Minh City's most recent former name, rendering it one of the younger cities in Asia at just over three hundred years old. By comparison, the current capital of Hanoi in the north has recently celebrated the 1000th anniversary of its founding.

As the lords of the Nguyen dynasty began ruling large portions of southern Vietnam, more and more Vietnamese settlers began to arrive from the north. A retreating and declining Cambodia, the region at the heart of the Khmer Empire, was simultaneously weakened by war with Thailand to the west. Therefore, the Khmer had few resources with which to defend the territory around Prey Nokor. Ultimately, they were unable to stop the encroachment of the arriving Vietnamese and the displacement of the Khmer became total. Soon, the Vietnamese had full control of all of today's southern Vietnam, extending through the Mekong Delta region to the Gulf of Thailand.

During this same period, a Chinese minority merchant class, having fled the conflicts and chaos of the post-Ming dynasty period in China, had established an encampment only a few miles from the village of Saigon. This became the trading community of *Cho Lon* ("big market"). The neighborhood still exists today and is known primarily as District 5 of Ho Chi Minh City, also known as "Chinatown." This trading center eventually became part of the expanding nearby settlement of Saigon, located mostly in what is today's District 1. This proximity of Cholon, as it is spelled in English, to the original Saigon, the business-mindedness of the Chinese merchant class, and commercial cooperation with the Vietnamese helped drive the entire area as an economic capital of the region. It also explains why a substantial population of Chinese is present in the city today.

Because of its hot climate, swampy land, mosquito problem, and other hardships attributable to its tropical geographic location, Saigon only grew slowly over the years. The imperial rulers of Vietnam in Hue maintained little continuing interest in the southern city, relegating it to secondary status as it struggled to grow through regional trade. Local power struggles also plagued the settlement. Soon, however, major European investment would help establish it as one of the primary commercial engines of Southeast Asia and a major commercial city recognized the world over.

French Colonialism

There had been French Catholic missionary presence since the 17th century; however, it was not until the middle of the 19th century under Napoleon III that France set its sights on colonializing Indochina. In 1859, the French military, helping France compete with other European powers in a race for global economic domination, had arrived in Vietnam. The period of colonialization had begun.

Overtaking and destroying the Saigon Citadel, an 18th century military fortress, the French captured and subsequently made Saigon the capital of what they called Cochinchina (the southern third of Vietnam). This became one of France's several Southeast Asian colonial territories. Some other Indochinese territories that eventually came under colonial French control included Laos, Cambodia, Annam (central Vietnam), and Tonkin (northern Vietnam). This was in addition to other French holdings around the world, including elsewhere in Asia, the South Pacific, Africa, South America, and the Caribbean.

French troops attacking the Saigon Citadel in 1859

After the establishment of French Saigon, the Mekong Delta and its water veins were opened to French colonialists for commercial exploitation. Saigon was on its way to becoming a significant pillar in the building of France's Indochinese empire. Capturing the city assisted France in rivaling the other European powers' overseas Asian empires, especially Britain and its various holdings, including Hong Kong, India (which included today's Pakistan and Bangladesh), and Singapore.

Autonomous French governors oversaw the organization of large plantations where native Vietnamese worked under harsh conditions. Rice and rubber were two of the primary commercial exports at the time, and their production was increasing as the colonial force became more entrenched. Saigon was becoming an important commercial capital in Southeast Asia for the French Empire.

Vietnamese emperors of the Nguyen dynasty remained as figureheads during this period, but they had little power. Vietnamese city names and streets were soon changed to French names. What is today's port city of Vung Tau (where Vietnamese "boat people" would later launch to flee the communists) was named Cap Saint-Jacques, and Dong Khoi Street, now the main boulevard through modern Ho Chi Minh City, was named Rue Catinat.

In the later 1800s, France's increasing influence in Saigon began to materialize in the city's architecture. Notre Dame Cathedral (and many other European-style churches), city hall, and the classic Saigon Central Post Office were all built during these early periods in French colonial architectural style. See the *Walking Tour* for more information about these landmarks.

A few decades later in 1929, there were 129,000 Vietnamese living in Saigon and approximately 12,000 French. Colonialization had hit its stride in Vietnam. The French attempted to justify their presence in Indochina as a "civilizing mission," and many schools and hospitals were indeed built during this period. The primary goal, however, was commercial exploitation and the acquisition of raw materials, enabling France to compete with other economic powers commercially on a global scale.

Colonialization had a major effect on the uniqueness and readability of today's Vietnamese language. Portuguese Catholic missionaries were the first to use Latin script for phonetically describing and representing the local language, a communication method that dates as far back as the 16th century. It was during the period of French rule, however, that the Roman alphabet was firmly established and taught as the written form and basis of the modern Vietnamese language. This eventually eliminated the Chinese-character based ancient Vietnamese script, consequently making the local language more readable for Westerners than other Asian languages. For more details, see the *Vietnamese Language* section of this book.

As you wander around Ho Chi Minh City today, the many colonial-era residences and other period buildings provide testament to the historical French colonial influence on the city. Sadly, many of the striking colonial-era buildings are now being demolished. Soon, only trace vestiges of the colonial period will remain. For now, there is still much obvious architectural evidence of the French empire to see across the entire city, but for how long is uncertain.

There are many other cultural remnants from this colonial period. From a culinary standpoint, you will see baguettes (the basis of the famous *banh mi* sandwich), cognac, a thriving coffee culture, snails, condensed milk, and several dishes and desserts of French influence, all with a twist of Vietnamese flavors born of a rich national culinary history of its own. This combination of national culinary influences has helped meld Vietnamese cuisine into one of the more unique and delicious gastronomic wonders of the world. See the *Cuisine of Ho Chi Minh City* section for more detail.

Many Vietnamese, especially scholars, resented the French presence and the subjugation of their people, and began meeting secretly to discuss how they could liberate Vietnam from the chains of colonialism. To the north, the first drumbeats of the resistance to come were beginning to figuratively echo through the countryside. Under a young man named Ho Chi Minh, the Indochinese Communist Party was formed in 1930 for the purposes of challenging foreign colonialism. The foundation of future conflict was beginning to take shape.

Japanese Occupation

In 1940, during the Second World War, the Japanese began their strategic occupation of Vietnam, including Saigon, as part of a broad application of imperialistic goals. Japan's primary purpose of the occupation, other than its own expansionist ambitions, was to prevent access to supplies and weapons by Japan's wartime enemy China through China's southern border. It also became a fallback position for the Japanese military after defeats in the Pacific, such as those suffered in the Philippines to the US. The French and the

Japanese coexisted in essentially a joint occupation of Vietnam for much of the war.

Soon after the surrender of the Japanese in the Second World War, the communist Viet Minh, a resistance faction with Ho Chi Minh as its leader, emerged as a political power in north and central Vietnam. Since France had been considerably weakened as a result of German occupation of its homeland and had less capacity to maintain its overseas colonies, the Allies installed British troops in Saigon to help enforce the Japanese surrender and withdrawal from southern Vietnam. The mutual Allied goal was to help the French regain colonial control of the country. However, it was no easy task for the British, as they faced street skirmishes and other countryside battles with the Viet Minh, who had been partners with the Allies in an attempt to end Japan's occupation, but were now attempting to take advantage of the power vacuum and assert itself in Saigon. It took until 1946 for the French to reestablish control over Vietnam, at which point the British were able to extricate themselves from the conflict.

The communist Viet Minh did not go quietly. They continued to battle the French throughout the country, who were determined to maintain Vietnam as a lasting colonial possession. The Viet Minh, to establish independence and gain its own control over Vietnam, enlisted peasants from the countryside and employed techniques of guerrilla warfare to battle the French. These incessant guerrilla attacks took their toll on the exhausted colonial forces. Finally, in 1954, the French were defeated and expelled from Vietnam at the siege and battle of Dien Bien Phu near the Chinese border.

The French exit, the leadership vacuum, and the prevailing uncertainty of the future resulted in Vietnam being divided along the 17th parallel into the two separate countries of North Vietnam and South Vietnam at the Geneva Conference in Switzerland, also held in 1954. This division was to be a temporary situation until national elections could be organized and held, enabling the country to reunify. Yet, there was no consensus as to what candidates could rule a unified Vietnam nor agreement as to how elections would be held.

Saigon had become the capital of the newly formed South Vietnam. The communist Viet Minh, who resisted and sought to end the division of the country, became the de facto leadership of North Vietnam and were installed in the capital of Hanoi. The creation of two separate incompatible countries created the foundation for the forthcoming arrival of the Americans and their quest to contain communism during the Cold War era. It set the stage for the conflict known in the West today as the Vietnam War, and known in Vietnam as the American War.

The United States in Vietnam

In the late 1950s, North Vietnamese guerrilla activity around Saigon recommenced. It was clear the communist Viet Minh had designs on the south and plans to control all of Vietnam using force. This aggression alarmed the United States, which feared the spread of communism as a continuing, global political threat. By 1960, the US had over seven hundred military advisors in South Vietnam to assist in the prevention of North Vietnamese communism spreading to and eventually dominating South Vietnam.

In 1962, United States President John F. Kennedy began significantly expanding US presence in Vietnam to keep the North Vietnamese at bay. His stated purpose was to prevent the "domino effect," a concept of containment proposed earlier by President Harry Truman, whereby countries fall to communism one-by-one in Southeast Asia and beyond as a line of dominoes falls, thereby increasing the aggregate threat of global communism against the US and other democracies. While this communist containment theory was put forth as part of the Truman Doctrine, some debate among scholars exists over who first used the actual term "falling dominoes."

Leaders in the US, mostly through the experience of the Second World War, had seen Germany, appeased at the Munich Conference in 1938, sweep through Western Europe one country at a time. These same leaders witnessed Japan occupy much of Asia during the same Second World War in a similar aggression. They watched the Soviet Union unilaterally install communist governments in Eastern Europe post-Second World War. These leaders were determined to prevent a similar falling of dominoes in Southeast Asia, including Cambodia, Laos, and Thailand. If Southeast Asia fell, they opined, perhaps next would be India and the rest of South Asia, and eventually the oil-rich Middle East. They were intent on containing communism and its primary authorities, namely China and the Soviet Union.

Many proponents of this containment theory believed that if Germany and Japan had been stopped earlier in their aggression during the 1930's, perhaps fewer lives—as many as sixty or seventy million perished—would have been lost during the Second World War and the global conflict would not have been as horrendously tragic as it turned out to be. In Truman's opinion, also a view shared by both President Dwight Eisenhower and President Kennedy to follow, Vietnam was the next domino in the struggle for world order. This time, the perceived communist aggression would be confronted early on.

There are those who vehemently disagreed with the domino theory. They believed that Vietnam was instead embroiled in a nationalist civil war and was neither a threat to the security of the US nor a battlefield proxy for a war against a global communist scourge. Those with this point of view insisted that the Americans should remain uninvolved militarily to avoid unnecessary bloodshed and to prevent risking further destabilization of the region.

Others insisted that regardless of the premise of the conflict, there was significant doubt whether South Vietnam could defend itself over the long haul, even with the aid of the United States. Therefore, the risk of a larger war involving China and the Soviet Union was too great to warrant an otherwise futile intervention.

The issues and the fierce debates surrounding these divergent opinions were complex, and attitudes on the subject still vary widely today. The domino theory, however, was deemed too great of a risk to leave unchecked, with the US leadership ultimately choosing to aid in the defense of South Vietnam believing that a communist Southeast Asia could not be tolerated and was a threat to Western security. Cold War battle lines had been drawn.

Ho Chi Minh, who had since become the President of North Vietnam, early on in his life had adopted communism as the basis for his own political views, and in keeping with the ideology of the Viet Minh, maintained it as the political foundation for the newly created North Vietnam.

In 1919, while in France as a youth traveling the world, Ho Chi Minh had petitioned for Vietnam's independence at the Versailles Peace Conference in Paris. Even though the petition went unrecognized, news of the event had reached his homeland. He emerged as a national political figure in Vietnam and a local hero in the country's fight for freedom against colonial oppression. Frustrated with the lack of response from Western democratic leaders, he then discovered and explored Marxist theory. He eventually joined the seemingly sympathetic French Communist Party when his pleas for assistance in independence from colonialism to the US and other European powers fell on deaf ears.

After some level of political involvement and futile colonial independence-lobbying in France, Ho Chi Minh soon left to spend time in Russia to further study communist ideology. By then, he was becoming a well-known figure in the global communist movement. He would eventually return to Vietnam to take over the leadership of the Viet Minh resistance group. The expulsion of the occupying Japanese and subsequently the colonial French led to his continued popularity. This ultimately propelled him to his position as President of North Vietnam. For more about the life of Ho Chi Minh, see the *Walking Tour* section of this book.

While Ho Chi Minh's political capital increased in the north, Saigon continued its governmental organizing as the capital of South Vietnam. Ngo Dinh Diem, a former cabinet member to the existing Vietnamese Emperor Bao Dai and a preferred choice of the Americans, became the first President of the fledgling nation. Diem's rule was one of strong anti-communist rhetoric, anti-rebellion tactics, and a focus on the security of the new southern nation.

Some claim Diem's policies strongly favored Catholics. Many Vietnamese viewed Catholicism as a remnant of European colonialism as millions continued to practice the religion after the departure of the French. This led to discontent among adherents of other religions prevalent in South Vietnam at the time, notably Buddhists, with followers fearing that under Diem their religion was being threatened. They complained of being treated with increasing hostility by the new leadership.

In 1963, the famous monk Thich Quang Duc horrified the world. He doused himself in gasoline and self-immolated on the streets of Saigon, bringing attention to the alleged mistreatment of Buddhists by the South Vietnamese regime. A memorial to the event worth visiting is in District 3; see *Other Sights*. This event brought worldwide attention to the military conflict escalating in Vietnam.

With the subsequent civil unrest, Diem imposed martial law on the streets of Saigon. Global condemnation of Diem, along with what was viewed as a deteriorating situation in South Vietnam, prompted the US to begin to distance itself from the leader.

Later the same year, South Vietnamese military generals plotted against President Diem. He was assassinated, along with his brother, in the Cholon section of Saigon after eight years of leadership. This led to instability in the South Vietnamese government and prompted yet a new power vacuum. Soon after in the same year, US President Kennedy was assassinated in Dallas. Acting Vice President Lyndon B. Johnson was sworn in as President after Kennedy's death and took the lead role regarding the interests of the US in Southeast Asia.

In 1964, a military ship named the USS Maddox was purportedly attacked in the Gulf of Tonkin off the coast of North Vietnam by North Vietnamese torpedo boat crews who had objected to the foreign presence off its shores. This was one of two separate alleged torpedo incidents. Some continue to doubt the veracity of the second attack and claim a lack of actual evidence that it took place. They instead cite US aggression in an attempt by the Americans to broaden the conflict and politically dominate the region into a more favorable geopolitical order. The details surrounding the alleged attacks are still debated to this day.

These incidents led the US Congress to pass the Gulf of Tonkin Resolution, granting President Johnson the use of conventional military force in Vietnam to maintain peace and security—without a formal declaration of war by the legislature. This broad measure would over time cause substantial expansion of the conflict.

Hostilities grew as the North Vietnamese continued to press for a unified Vietnam under communism. Its communist ally and counterpart in South Vietnam, the National Liberation Front, also known as the Viet Cong, continued to exert pressure on the American-supported South Vietnamese regime. Saigon soon began to experience the realities of an encroaching and burgeoning war.

For example, in August of 1964, a bomb exploded on the fifth floor of the famed Caravelle Hotel. This hotel in downtown Saigon was where many war correspondents, including well-known news anchor Walter Cronkite, would later stay and witness battle scenes on the outskirts of the city from its rooftop. This bomb was allegedly targeting foreign journalists and was one of many such bombings.

In 1965 after Diem's assassination, there were several other temporary leaders and coup attempts within the South Vietnamese government. This fractured leadership in Saigon played a major role in the inability of the US-South Vietnamese coalition to organize effectively and to gain broad support of the Vietnamese people. The conditions within the defense effort of South Vietnam began to deteriorate significantly. As the reports of falling confidence came in from his generals and advisors, President Johnson determined that the only way the North Vietnamese could be kept at bay would be via the presence and subsequent increase of US ground troops in Vietnam. These ground troops began to engage in deadly battles with North Vietnamese troops in rural areas of Vietnam. The war became one of total US involvement.

Eventually, after several interim leaders, Nguyen Van Thieu became the second official President of South Vietnam. He would serve in such capacity in Saigon for the next ten years.

By 1966, there were over a million US troops in Vietnam defending against the spread of communism and its proclaimed corresponding threat to global democracy. Most new military personnel arriving by air transited through Saigon's Tan Son Nhat airport, the same airport used for arrivals to Ho Chi Minh City today. Immediately upon disembarkation, they faced the prospect of action, even while being shuttled from the plane. Young soldiers from large cities and little towns all over America were now heavily installed throughout South Vietnam, trained and equipped for fierce battle.

The war in Vietnam became significant because of the heavy journalist presence and the use of video equipment to capture the intensity and drama of the conflict. Footage of the war came right into America's living rooms, exposing Americans at home to the harsh, horrific realities of battle and putting a human face to the war's casualties. Eventually, the television coverage and the continuing journalism largely critical of the US would lead the American public to turn against the nation's military presence in Vietnam.

Other war correspondents stayed at the Rex Hotel, also in downtown Saigon, where the American military command had a significant presence and held its daily press briefings on the roof. Over time, some journalists dubbed these briefings the Five O'clock Follies because of their developing cynicism; many reporters in Saigon covering the conflict disbelieved favorable reports coming from the field, especially after talking directly with US soldiers. These journalists claimed soldiers often gave accounts conflicting with the statements of military leadership, including material information such as casualty numbers, as well as details about what was actually occurring in the combat zones.

Meanwhile, in the United States, campus protests against the US presence in Indochina expanded significantly, including in Berkeley, California; Madison, Wisconsin; and at Kent State University in Ohio, where, in one of the more notorious and tragic incidents of the war, the National Guard shot and killed four students after violent protests. These protests would only increase in size and number in the coming years as American casualties mounted abroad.

In 1968, amidst what appeared to be a continuing military stalemate, the North Vietnamese launched the surprise Tet Offensive, so named because it was executed during Vietnam's Tet Lunar New Year holiday celebrations, a time when most of the south had expected a period of cease-fire. These attacks were widespread, engulfing nearly every provincial capital in South Vietnam. The American embassy in Saigon was attacked and briefly taken over; elsewhere, several top South Vietnamese leaders were assassinated.

The event however was ultimately a military victory for the combined forces of the South Vietnamese and the US. It took a serious toll on the anti-communists. Yet, historians often identify it as the psychological turning point of the war in favor of the North, as many southern cities were devastated because of these surprise attacks. Confidence in a victory against the communists began to wane, especially with the American television-watching public who had witnessed much of the massive bloodshed on the nightly news.

Later in 1968, feeling the overwhelming pressure of the war, a fiercely divided constituency, and the lack of acceptable alternatives for ending the conflict, President Johnson chose not to run for reelection. The quagmire appeared insurmountable.

In 1969, President Richard Nixon, after promising a peaceful end to the war during his 1968 election campaign, announced the beginning of what he called the Vietnamization of the war. He ordered accelerated training of more South Vietnamese troops and the gradual withdrawal of US troops in a quest for "peace with honor," and to quell the rising tide of protest and decreasing confidence within the US over the necessity of involvement in Vietnam. During this year, an ailing and no longer militarily active Ho Chi Minh died. He did not live to see the nation's eventual reunification.

After years of continued battle, suffering, and death in the Vietnamese countryside, there seemed to be no end in sight to the war on either side. As of 1972, peace talks and negotiations between North Vietnam and South Vietnam continued to stall. Much of the impasse revolved around North Vietnamese negotiating with the United States for a cease-fire in exchange for the return of American Prisoners-of-

War (POWs), without the direct involvement of the South Vietnamese leadership. There also continued to be stark disagreement over peace terms. Many believed the US was engaging in negotiations in an attempt to extricate itself from the conflict. The South Vietnamese resented and furiously objected to what they saw as a betrayal of accepted common ideals and political expediency on behalf of the United States.

During the slow-moving negotiations in 1972, exercising his remaining escalation options to bring the war to an end, President Nixon initiated the Christmas bombing of Hanoi, breathing renewed confidence into the defense of South Vietnam and its hopes for victory and continued existence without the threat of communism. The resulting devastation in Hanoi, combined with the stalemate on the battlefield, severely hampered the North Vietnamese collective political will for unifying Vietnam through force under communism.

Soon after, the Paris Peace Accords were signed, resulting in a cease-fire, a return of POWs, and the continued division of North Vietnam and South Vietnam as separate countries. Seemingly, the US had achieved its stated goal of keeping South Vietnam free from communist rule. By 1973, all American troops had been withdrawn from Vietnam. Although 58,000 United States military personnel had died during the war, "peace with honor" had been achieved. Saigon would remain a national capital safe from communism.

This "peace" would not last. In 1974, President Nixon was forced to resign from office because of the Watergate scandal that had erupted in the United States. Consequently, Vice President Gerald Ford became the new US President. President Ford reaffirmed his support for South Vietnam to then President Thieu in a personal letter.

Also in 1974, sensing American political instability and a window of opportunity, the North Vietnamese leadership authorized more attacks on South Vietnam and reinitiated their plans for the unification of Vietnam under communism in conflict with the terms of the Paris Peace Accords. During this time, without American military forces on the ground and no military personnel spending money locally, the South Vietnamese economy had begun to suffer substantially. It was ill-prepared for another wave of North Vietnamese attacks.

In January of 1975, the US Congress voted to rebuff President Ford and stopped providing funding for the South Vietnamese defense effort. America's congressional leadership, along with much of the American public, had grown tired of the conflict and did not have the political will to continue to support the South Vietnamese, especially financially, and left them to their own devices. This decision served as a "green light" for the North Vietnamese. It signaled the opportunity they had been waiting for to militarily roll through South Vietnam, which no longer had the support of the US or significant access to its resources. Without international assistance, the South Vietnamese were easily overwhelmed by the North Vietnamese communists who still enjoyed major, unwavering support from the Soviet Union and China.

This in turn led to the fall of Saigon in April of 1975. In its climax, North Vietnamese soldiers in Russian-made tanks broke through the gates of the South Vietnamese headquarters, today known as Reunification Palace. All remaining US personnel, mostly administrative employees and other civilians, were airlifted to safety by helicopter from the American Embassy in Saigon. Back in the US, those who had fought admirably to protect South Vietnam from the communist North Vietnamese could only watch the tragic events unfold from their homes on television. Surviving American soldiers, many of which already were beginning to feel the effects of combat-related post-traumatic stress disorder, were dumbfounded as the North Vietnamese flag was hoisted over Saigon. The nation of South Vietnam was no more.

North Vietnamese soldiers blasted through the gated South Vietnamese Presidential Headquarters in Soviet-made tanks like this one, now on display at Reunification Palace, in the final hours of the Fall of Saigon.

In 1976, a reunified communist Vietnam, following the lead of the Soviet Union with cities named Leningrad and Stalingrad after their communist leaders, officially changed Saigon's name to Ho Chi Minh City as enacted by the new national government in Hanoi. Saigon itself as an official city name was also no more.

Modern Ho Chi Minh City

The years after Saigon fell were difficult ones. Many of the South Vietnamese men that remained in Ho Chi Minh City after the collapse were sent to reeducation camps. Many of South Vietnam's former leaders that were unable to escape were either killed or committed suicide. Much property was confiscated. The former South Vietnam's economy, significantly dependent on US military personnel spending, was in shambles. Over three million South Vietnamese left the country soon after the war as refugees. Tragically, as many as five hundred thousand "boat people" are thought to have perished at sea as they attempted to escape.

Widespread famine occurred throughout Vietnam after the war, especially during the years 1979-1982. In 1985, the established Vietnamese government realized the Soviet-style centrally planned economy was not working as designed, and consequently reopened the country to tourism in an effort to affect a financial turnaround. These economic reforms were part of a new set of policies known throughout Vietnam as *Doi Moi* (meaning a "new change").

In 1995, Vietnam reestablished relations with the US and began an effort at reconciliation. US President Bill Clinton visited Ho Chi Minh City and a US Consulate was established at the site of the original wartime South Vietnam US Embassy.

In 2000, the first of several US-Vietnam bilateral trade agreements was established. In 2006, US President George W. Bush granted Vietnam permanent normal trade relations status, paving the way for Vietnam's entry into the World Trade Organization (WTO). In 2007, Vietnam became the 150th member of the WTO.

In 2010, the fifty-four-story Bitexco Financial Tower was completed and inaugurated in Ho Chi Minh City; it was the tallest building in Vietnam at the time. In 2011, the Keangnam Hanoi Landmark Tower superseded it in height, giving the title back to Hanoi. Still, the modern era of skyline development in Ho Chi Minh City had begun.

In 2014, along with a new free trade agreement with the European Union, the US-Vietnamese trade agreement expanded further, and the first McDonald's, Starbucks, and Burger Kings began to appear in the city, gradually increasing in number. By 2016, a rapidly developing Ho Chi Minh City had a combined total of fifteen Burger King and McDonald's locations, and several Starbucks and other international coffee outlets. While of little culinary interest to tourists, the appearance of Western chain restaurants is perhaps an indicator of Ho Chi Minh City's future commercial direction. With hope, however, the country will continue to maintain its unique traditions and ancient culture.

In 2016, in a historic move, US President Barack Obama visited Vietnam and lifted an arms embargo against the country, allowing for the sale of lethal weapons to the Vietnamese government. Many see this as perhaps a response to China's controversial claims over islands in the South China Sea. In 2017, US President Donald

Trump visited Vietnam and additional aid was provided to the country in 2018. These visits and agreements clearly indicate Western interests of new allies to achieve political balance in the region.

For many Americans and other international tourists, the mere mention of the name "Vietnam" conjures images of the tragic war that once engulfed this nation more than forty years ago. For most Vietnamese however, the war is distant history, and they are working hard to forge a positive and prosperous future for themselves, their families, and their fellow citizens. For now, the future holds much promise for Vietnam. An estimated five million international travelers are visiting Ho Chi Minh City in 2016, a number that grows every year.

Before 1100s ●------
Champa civilization presence
in region, mostly swampland

1100s - 1500s --------------------------------
Khmer people from Angkor dominate the area,
settlement in future location of Saigon called "Prey Nokor"

1600s ----------------------------
Vietnamese settlers from the north begin to arrive,
Khmer presence gradually pushed out

○ **1698** --------------
Officials in Vietnamese
imperial capital of Hue
annex area,

Annexation results in
birth of Vietnamese
settlement that will
become Saigon

1700s --------------------------------
Chinese merchants and Ming dynasty refugees arrive,
More northern Vietnamese continue to arrive,
Early European missionary work present in the area

○ **1859** --------------------------------
Colonial French arrive in Vietnam,
French military attacks and captures Saigon

Late 1800s - Early 1900s ---
French colonial architecture booms in Saigon,
Business of colonialism in Indochina hits stride

○ **1911** --------------
Young Ho Chi Minh first
travels to Europe and
engages in politics

○ **1923** --------------
Ho Chi Minh travels to
Russia and studies at the
Lenin Institute

○ **1930** ----------
Ho Chi Minh forms
Indochinese Communist
Party from Hong Kong

○ **1940** --------------------------------
Second World War arrives in Saigon with Japanese occupation

○ **1945** --
Japan surrenders to Allies after atom bombs dropped on Japan,
Ho Chi Minh declares independence for Vietnam,
Viet Minh emerges as anti-foreigner communist guerrilla faction

○ **1946** --------------
With British assistance,
French re-establish
colonial Vietnam

○ **1954** --------------------------------
Defeat and exit of French at Dien Bien Phu,
Geneva Conference divides Vietnam into two countries at the 17th parallel,
Saigon becomes capital of South Vietnam

○ **1955** --------------------------------------
Ngo Dinh Diem becomes first President of South Vietnam
after appointment to Prime Minister from acting Emperor
of Vietnam Bao Dai,

Nearly one million North Vietnamese choose to evacuate
and settle into South Vietnam before borders are sealed

○ **1962** --------------
US President Kennedy,
citing domino theory,
expands US presence in
Vietnam to prevent fall of
South Vietnam to North
Vietnamese communists

○ **1963** --------------------------------
Buddhist monk Thich Quang Duc self-immolates in
event that is captured on video and viewed globally,

South Vietnam President Diem assassinated by South
Vietnamese Generals,

US President Kennedy assassinated in Dallas,
Lyndon Johnson becomes US President

○ **1964** --------------
Gulf of Tonkin torpedo
incident,

US Congress passes Gulf
of Tonkin Resolution
giving President Johnson
authority to escalate
conflict as necessary

1965
Heavy presence in South Vietnam
of Viet Minh-supported guerrilla
arm known as Viet Cong,

US ground forces enter Vietnam
to counter expanding threat,

US forces and Viet Cong guerrillas
engage in combat for first time in
the Ia Drang Valley

1966
Over a million US ground troops
have entered Vietnam

1968
Tet Offensive results in large-scale,
brutal combat all throughout South Vietnam

President Johnson announces he will
not seek re-election

1969
Newly reelected US President Richard Nixon takes over as Commander in Chief,

Announces Vietnamization of conflict and gradual US troop withdrawal

1972
Peace talks take center
stage over continued
stalemate,

Christmas bombing of
Hanoi puts pressure on
North Vietnamese,

President Nixon
reelected in largest
landslide in US
election history

1973
US and North Vietnam
sign Paris Peace Accords,

Vietnam will remain
partitioned, all US
troops withdrawn

1974
Watergate causes
President Nixon to resign,

US President Gerald Ford
sworn in

1975
US Congress votes to stop funding South Vietnam war effort,
North Vietnamese see opportunity and militarily roll through
hobbled South Vietnam,

Saigon falls and remaining US consulate personnel evacuated,

South Vietnam ceases to exist

1976
Vietnam reunified as communist nation,
Saigon is renamed Ho Chi Minh City

1985
Vietnam announces Doi Moi economic
reforms to jumpstart sputtering economy

1995
US President Bill Clinton visits Ho Chi
Minh City - first US President to do so
post-Vietnam War, establishes relations
and US Consulate in former South
Vietnam embassy location

2006
US President George W. Bush grants Vietnam
permanent trade relations status

2007
Vietnam joins World
Trade Organization

2014
Vietnam signs European
Union free trade agreement,
Expands US trade agreement

2016
US President Barack Obama
lifts sales of arms embargo
on Vietnam, expanding
relationship with Vietnam

Arriving to the City

Most likely you will be arriving in Ho Chi Minh City at Tan Son Nhat International Airport (IATA airport code SGN). International flights arrive at International Terminal 2. This new terminal, slated for further expansion in 2016, was completed in 2007. Domestic flights arrive and depart at Terminal 1.

Tan Son Nhat Airport is Vietnam's largest and handles approximately twenty-five million passengers per year. French colonialists built the airport in the 1930s, which originally consisted of unpaved runways. US aid helped build a paved runway in the 1950s, and US and South Vietnamese Air Force units used the airport extensively during the Vietnam War. Many young servicemen from the United States arrived for their tours of duty at this airport. It is only four miles to the north of the city center. While a new, larger international airport is in the planning stages farther outside the city, it continues to face delays; it will probably be a long way off into the future before it sees its first landing.

Upon arrival, you will first pass through immigration where you will show your passport and visa. You will then pick up your baggage at baggage claim, after which it will then go through a required bag screening machine operated by Vietnamese customs officials. Every piece of luggage collected through baggage claim must go through this screening process. You will load your bags yourself onto the screening machine. Please be aware of any customs declaration requirements, such as foreign currency limits, tax-free import limits (such as alcohol—smaller amounts are ok), banned substances, and other disallowed items. Customs officials will select some bags for additional screening.

The cheapest way to travel into the city is by bus, although this is probably an acceptable choice for only the most frugal of travelers. Bus #152 will cost under one dollar (you will need local currency) and will take you to the Ben Thanh Market area where many hotels are located. The city center is only a few blocks from this point. The bus is scheduled to run every twenty minutes during the morning and afternoon until 6 p.m. Keep in mind that the likelihood of hot weather might make this choice, and the subsequent walk to your hotel carrying bags, somewhat unpleasant.

Ideally, make arrangements with your hotel for pickup, despite it being more expensive than other options. Your driver will be waiting for you with your name on a placard outside of baggage claim. Obtain the name and license plate of the driver in advance to ensure you get into the proper vehicle.

If you take a taxi, realize that there are many unauthorized taxis at the airport looking for passengers. Some of these are trying to make a few extra bucks for their families, while others are unscrupulous and will be targeting tourists perhaps to cheat them with high taxi fees, and in extreme and rare cases, to potentially rob arriving tourists (even using fake placards with real names of arriving passengers). There are also legitimate taxis with significantly higher-than-standard rates looking to capitalize on unsuspecting tourists.

Two taxi companies that are normally reliable and less likely to use rigged meters (unfortunately a common taxi practice throughout Vietnam) are Vinasun (white taxis) and Mai Linh (green taxis). Be aware that some scheming taxi drivers will mock up their vehicles to look like those of these companies or wear fake badges from these companies. Be sure to look closely at the vehicle and its logos, and only enter the vehicle at the designated taxi pickup location.

Separate taxi companies have separate taxi lines. As you exit the terminal, an official looking person may direct you to a given taxi line. This does not mean you must get in that specific taxi line. Be sure to stand in the taxi line of a company you are comfortable receiving a ride from. Vinasun and Mai Linh have their own taxi lines and they usually have a company representative around that will help you hail a taxi from their particular company, or you might need to walk to their designated pickup points. You will need to be persistent in your taxi company selection as there are people who will try to wave you into the more expensive airport vehicle lines, but it is recommended that you use one of these two suggested companies and queue in their corresponding taxi lines.

Typical taxi fees from the airport to the city center are 150,000 to 200,000 VND (around $7-$10 USD). Sometimes there may be a nominal fee for luggage, but it shouldn't be more than 250,000 VND total. Be sure to negotiate the rate in advance or make sure that the meter is on before the taxi departs the airport.

Also, if you do not have Vietnamese dong, the local currency, obtain some at one of several ATMs throughout the airport. Try to obtain a minimum of one or two million dong ($50-$100) for pocket money. You might be able to pay your fare with US dollars or other foreign currency, but it is unlikely that you will get the appropriate exchange rate.

Another option is to use Uber or other ride-sharing services from the airport. An account set up in advance and Internet access is necessary to use these services. With Uber, the rate is set by the master Uber system over the Internet, so there is no risk of a rigged meter. Your credit card is charged, therefore no cash need change hands. You can also follow the route on your smart device via GPS to ensure you are headed to your desired destination. At the time of the writing of this book, Uber is significantly cheaper than taxis as the young company looks to obtain market share. Be aware that some of these ride-sharing services are facing regulatory problems in Vietnam. There is the unpleasant possibility of being delayed or experiencing some other hassle if you are in a vehicle during a crackdown of these services.

Luggage storage is available for a fee at the airport if needed.

Districts of the City

Ho Chi Minh City is administratively divided into a series of districts (*quan*), each unique in character. This partitioning makes it easier to determine where things are located, for general purposes of addressing, and for civil management by the local government. For increased specificity, each of these districts is broken down further into subdistricts, typically numbering in the ten to twenty range per district. These subdistricts are called wards (*phuong*). Addresses usually have the district and ward as part of the address structure (example "q1 p4").

These are important units from an administrative standpoint. For example, if you are the victim of robbery in ward 6 in a given district, you must go to that particular police station to report it, not the one nearest to where you are staying. Sometimes, wards even have names rather than numbers, such as "Ben Nghe" in District 1. If you mail anything to Ho Chi Minh City or within Ho Chi Minh City, use both the district and the ward in the addressing of the item for a greater chance of its arrival.

Ho Chi Minh City has twenty-four of these separate districts. Twelve of these are referred to by a number, and twelve others have proper names. Nineteen are within the core of the city, while five others are more out-lying and suburban. Most of the districts nearest downtown are known by a number. For example, District 1 covers the primary downtown area and is where tourists spend most of their time, as it contains the more popular accommodations.

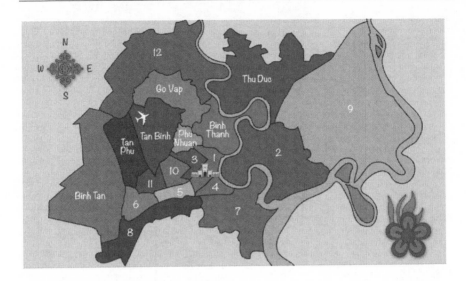

Here is a description of several (but not all) of these districts, especially the ones you are more likely to spend time in.

District 1. This is the primary central district downtown where all the towering buildings, government centers, major hotels, and many of the major tourist sites are located. These include Notre Dame Cathedral, the Opera House, Central Post Office, Reunification Palace, the US Consulate, and several of the city's top historical and art museums. The city's most famous streets such as Dong Khoi, Le Loi, Nguyen Hue, and Hai Ba Trung are all located here. It is the most cosmopolitan area of the city, where one can find both top-notch Vietnamese and international restaurants, high-end shopping, nightlife, cafes, and some of the city's finest hotels. The backpacker areas of Pham Ngu Lao and Bui Vien within District 1 can provide some of the best options for budget hotels and dining.

Tourists spend a majority of their time in District 1. It is also known as the "Saigon" district because of its historical roots, the location of the original town of Saigon, and the early Saigon Citadel where the modern city began.

District 2. On the other side of the Saigon River from District 1, District 2 was historically home to the poorer residents of Ho Chi Minh City because of its separation from the city by the river. Today it is becoming one of the wealthier districts because of metropolitan expansion and significant investment geared towards higher living standards. The modernization is an effort to be more like a Hong Kong or Singapore with the quality of life to match. Many modern and international restaurants are found in District 2, as well as high-rent residences and golf courses. This area is a favorite among professional expats.

District 3. Adjacent to District 1 and with a sizable amount of colonial charm (it was a favorite residential district of many French colonialists), this area is also a favorite of expats. It has several tourist destinations and is blessed with a roster of excellent restaurants, enthralling nightlife, and classic coffee shops frequented by tourists and locals alike. There are several pagodas to visit here and several remaining French villas from the colonial period (although the number is decreasing quite rapidly). There is some heavy traffic in this part of the city, but for the most part it is quieter than District 1. This makes it ideal for more apartment-style and longer stay accommodations for tourists where peacefulness trumps the convenience of District 1, while still being only ten to fifteen minutes away from the city center.

District 4. This is the smallest of the urban districts. It is where the Saigon Port is located. Locals sometimes refer to this area as a "gangster area," and not in a favorable way. In general, this is probably not the location for tourists to wander, although *Oc Street* (Snail Street) of culinary fame is located here.

District 5. This is Ho Chi Minh City's Chinatown. There are an estimated six hundred thousand Chinese living here, many of whose ancestors immigrated to Vietnam when the Ming dynasty fell in the 1600s; many took local wives and had children that identified more with Chinese than Vietnamese culture. Many others came during other periods of political strife in China such as the civil war period of the 1940s, or merely as merchants looking for new business opportunities. There are many markets here, including the "big market," or Cholon. It is more traditional in architecture and way of life, and English is less spoken here.

District 6. This area also makes up part of the Cholon Chinatown district and has much spillover from District 5. There is not much to see for most tourists in this district, except perhaps for some obscure restaurant finds.

District 7. With a Los Angeles-like feel and wide, palm tree-lined streets, more cars than motorbikes, hip streetside cafes, and luxurious high-rises, this up-and-coming corner of the city doesn't feel culturally much like Vietnam. The Phu My Hung sub-district is especially a center of wealth with its million-dollar residences, Western-style grocery stores, and a multitude of international and upscale local restaurants. This neighborhood is popular with expat families from both the East and the West. It is a considerable distance from here to District 1, perhaps as much as thirty minutes or more by hired car.

District 8. There is little in the way of tourist sites here. There are several outdoor barbecue restaurants lined up in this area, with high flames and plenty of goat, chicken, snails, and seafood smoking over hot charcoal.

District 9. This district, on the opposite side from downtown past District 2, is remote and does not have much with respect to tourist interest, save for some golf courses. It is the largest of the Ho Chi Minh City districts.

District 10. A densely populated district, there are many markets, pagodas, and street food shops in the area. A significant student population exists here because of cheaper rents and nearby schools. There are shopping streets here where an entire street can specialize in a single item (although this is not a concept unique to District 10).

District 11. This district is a considerable distance from the city center on the opposite side of District 10. There is not much in the way of tourist sites here.

District 12. Remote and on the northern edge of the city past the airport, this is an industrial district that also plays host to multiple fledgling high-tech businesses.

District Tan Binh. This is the district containing the airport. Much local city life can be experienced on the streets here, including clusters of local restaurants.

District Binh Thanh (yes, this is different from Tan Binh and Binh Tan). Locals enjoy outdoor, riverside dining at Thanh Da Island located here. It is the location of the Binh Quoi Tourist Villages (see the *Where to Eat* section), which have large, bountiful Vietnamese buffets and pleasant grounds to visit. The feel is similar to the Mekong Delta. Live traditional music and great picture taking is a highlight here. Binh Quoi is visited by tourists and locals alike.

District Binh Tan. This is primarily a working-class neighborhood far from the city center.

District Phu Nhuan. Geographically the most central of Ho Chi Minh City's districts, it is wedged between District 1, District 3, and the airport. There are tombs of former emperors here, pagodas, a mosque, and many coffee shops and restaurants to visit.

District Go Vap. This is primarily a local residential district with heavy traffic and little English spoken.

District Tan Phu. Approximately forty-five minutes from downtown, this newer district (formerly a part of Tan Binh) has some local dining but a lack of compelling tourist sights.

District Thu Duc. Once divided to create District 2 and District 9, it is now known for the colonial-built wholesale Thu Duc Market and Thu Duc Church.

Ten Great Experiences

If you only have a few days in Ho Chi Minh City, or want to have a comprehensive set of experiences during your visit, here are ten ideas that will maximize your time and give you a glimpse of the best that the "seductress of the river," otherwise known as Ho Chi Minh City, has to offer. You should be able to experience all of these at least in some capacity on a forty-eight-hour speed tour, but they can also be spread out over a week or so on longer visits to enjoy each one more completely.

In no particular order:

1. **Street food hopping.** The street food scene in Ho Chi Minh City is as diverse as it is exotic, like no other, and only rivaled by a few other cities in the world. From fire-grilled snails and squid, stacks of fresh rice paper "roll food" layered in flavor, boiling kettles of spicy broth and noodles, to smoking bananas smothered in warm coconut sauce, the street food experience is an absolute must. You will find hundreds of local dishes cooked and served curbside, often from smoldering hot coals, and usually costing only a pittance. And since these flaming grills can be found on practically every block citywide, you won't have to go far to find something to try. See the *Where to Eat* section for more details on where and how to attack the street food scene.

2. **Dining in a beautiful restaurant.** On the opposite side of the spectrum from Ho Chi Minh City's spectacular street food landscape are the many stunning, beautifully decorated fine dining establishments throughout the city. From colonial French villas to hand-carved teakwood tables and candlelit charm, you will feel like you are eating inside an elegantly romantic and aristocratic setting within the Southeast Asian jungle. This distinctly Vietnamese ambience, combined with warm and friendly service and some of the finest and most beautifully prepared dishes in all of Southeast Asia, will make for a grand and memorable experience. See the *Where to Eat* section for more details.

3. **Coffee shop culture.** Vietnam is the world's second largest coffee producer behind Brazil. It is no wonder it has a vibrant coffee shop culture. Ho Chi Minh City's unique history has given way to both classic and modern coffee shops, live music cafes, social coffee houses, entrepreneurial coffee shops, themed coffee houses, and some that are purely visions of spectacular, flower-garden-by-the-stream beauty. To not visit a couple of these would be a sad omission from your trip. See the *Coffee Shop Culture* section for more details.

4. **An intense, motorized two-wheel bike tour.** There are a multitude of "bike tours" where you ride on the back of a motorbike with a local, licensed guide navigating the urban madness, while making several stops in an up-close, on-the-streets Ho Chi Minh City experience. While it can be hair-raising at times whirring through traffic on the back of your tour guide's bike, it will undoubtedly be one of the highlights of your trip. There are historical tours, city tours, night tours, day tours, and extremely popular and adventuresome food tours, where you will hit several top, hidden local food establishments trying various local dishes and delicacies, zooming across town between courses. See *Tours and Activities* for more details and options.

5. **Reunification Palace.** No trip to Ho Chi Minh City would be complete without a close look at the brutal, tragic, and politicized historical record that still heavily populates its streets. The must-see site is the former "palace" that after its completion served as the office of the President of South Vietnam during the nation's existence. The palace is still maintained as it was in the 1960s and 1970s. This is the famous building where North Vietnamese tanks rolled through the gates in April 1975 serving as the climactic moment in the fall of Saigon. See *Major Sights* for more details.

6. **A walk down Dong Khoi Street.** At over six hundred meters long and at the heart of Ho Chi Minh City's District 1 urban and commercial center, this street has been the center of city life since French colonial days. Then it was known as the Rue Catinat, and during the existence of South Vietnam it was known as the entertainment-filled Tu Do Street. Stretching from the Saigon River to Notre Dame Cathedral, this main city artery passes the Opera

House, long-famous hotels, classic coffee shops, boutique shopping, alluring restaurants, and many addresses of historical significance. For more detail and a guided walk, see the *Walking Tour* section.

7. **A drink at a classic rooftop bar.** Step back in time to one of several historical and noteworthy rooftop bars or one of the modern equivalents that dot the city with views from the sky. Old-style rooftop bars like at the Caravelle Hotel, riverside bars like at the Majestic Hotel, the modern rooftop club-bars like that of the Sheraton or the hot, relatively new open-air Chill Skybar are all fun and unique local experiences. See the *Nightlife* section for more details.

8. **Nighttime people watching on Bui Vien.** For an electric experience, visit "foreigner central" Bui Vien Street. Grab a chair and a cheap, cold local beer and prepare for some fascinating people-watching and intense nightlife. Fire breathers, street peddlers of all sorts, dried squid delicacy bike carts, enterprising locals, and good-time citizens from the around the world will stroll back-and-forth on this street nightly, passing bright neon signs, energetic bars (some with live music), night clubs, local Vietnamese "barbecue" joints, street food vendors, massage parlors, and boutique (some seedy) hotels. If a New Orleans Bourbon Street-like atmosphere "Saigon Style" sounds compelling, then surely you will have a blast on Bui Vien.

9. **A morning walk through Ben Thanh Market.** The colonial French established this large, lively marketplace. It is one of the longest surviving landmarks in the city. It's best to visit in the morning, not only to avoid the afternoon heat, but because the early hours are prime time for the frenzied atmosphere of seafood and meat market stalls that wrap up their business well before noon. Live fish, crab, lobster, frog, snake, and every part imaginable of pigs, cows, and poultry are fresh and out for display. Noodles, take-home desserts, dried ingredients, and a wide assortment of local fruits and vegetables are abundantly available throughout the day. The retail, gift, and souvenir sections can also be visited at any time. You can grab a meal or enjoy one of the famous "rainbow" beverages while you wander. See more details in the *Major Sights* section.

10. **A relaxing massage.** After a long, crazy, hot day, a relaxing rub down from soft, local fingers in the refuge and solitude of a massage chamber is an excellent way to unwind and collect yourself. Eliminate your aches and pains in peaceful bliss and you will be glowing in time for a wonderful dinner. There are many varieties of massage available throughout the city. Compared with Western prices for an equivalent experience, the cost is unbeatable. For more information, see the *Massage* section.

Walking Tour

This introductory, get-acquainted walking tour starts with the buzz of Ho Chi Minh City's famous rectangular Ben Thanh Market, winds you through historic streets and landmarks, and finishes at the end of venerated and fanciful Dong Khoi Street near the Saigon River. The tour is entirely within District 1 (see the *Districts of Ho Chi Minh City* section for more information about the city's districting system). It is designed to give a new visitor to Ho Chi Minh City an orientation to the historic parts of the city in a couple of hours, as well as a close-up look at its ever-changing and compelling present. This overview activity will enable you to appropriately allocate time for the rest of your visit based on your discoveries and interests. The tour also ensures that you see several significant sights of the city, making it especially useful for shorter visits.

The tour is best done early in the morning when the activity at Ben Thanh Market (point #1 on the walking tour map) is at its most frenetic. Heavy market activity starts to wind down around 11 a.m., especially as the fresh supply of seafood and meat products begins to dwindle. Getting to the market early is important for the full and best experience. It is also an ideal time to beat the onset of the day's heat.

This walking tour can be done at other times if you are under time constraints, as most of the rest of the tour outside of the market is not time-dependent. The tour can be completed in an hour on a brisk walk with little stopping. If you linger at sites or choose a slower pace, it can take two hours or more. So put on the sunscreen, don a hat and sunglasses, and let's get things rolling.

Ho Chi Minh City Walking Tour

Points of Interest:

1 - Ben Thanh Market (tour starts here)
2 - Corner of Le Loi
3 - L'Usine
4 - Taka Plaza "Hem"
5 - Liberty Citypoint Hotel
6 - City Hall
7 - Ho Chi Minh Statue
8 - Union Square Shopping Mall
9 - Vincom Center
10 - Helicopter Platform
11 - Notre Dame Basilica and Statue of Mary
12 - Post Office
13 - Continental Hotel
14 - Bombing Memorial
15 - Old Opium Refinery
16 - Caravelle Hotel
17 - Opera House
18 - Sheraton Hotel
19 - Mao Thi Buoi "Hem"
20 - Reverie Hotel, Times Square Building
21 - Majestic Hotel (tour ends here)
22 - Bitexco (point of reference, not part of tour)

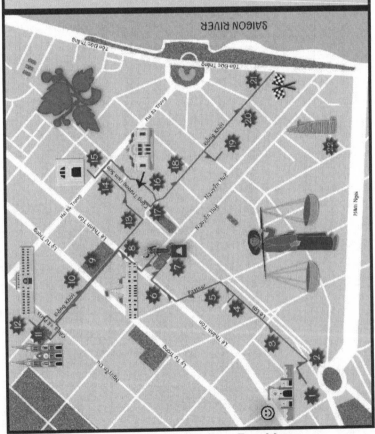

Ho Chi Minh City Walking Tour Map

After making your way to the starting point of the tour at Ben Thanh Market (#1), enter at any gate to begin the exhilarating market experience. Ben Thanh Market is the soul of street vendor selling in Ho Chi Minh City, and it has been for well over a century. As you wander through the stalls, you will find souvenirs, exotic regional food, unique beverages, locally made traditional and modern apparel, unusual and chic shoes, regional coffee bean varieties, chopsticks, tea sets, art, and much more. In the morning hours, the fresh food vendors are hard at work cutting meat and preparing seafood products. In the butcher stalls for example, you may witness some gruesome scenes. Other busy vendors are presenting fruits, vegetables, herbs, spices, and a wide variety of other fresh food products to their customers. Welcome to the heartbeat of Ho Chi Minh City's grand culinary extravaganza.

In the 17th century, Ho Chi Minh City's original markets were down by the Saigon River not far from here. Soon after arriving in the city, the colonializing French established a covered market in a location a few blocks down nearby Ham Nghi Street towards the river. The French called this marketplace *Les Halles Centrales*. Locals began calling it *Cho Ben Thanh* (Ben Thanh Market) because it was a marketplace (*cho*), close to a wharf (*ben*), and near the original Gia Dinh Citadel (*thanh*). Fire destroyed the original marketplace in 1869.

A second market existed over on Nguyen Hue Boulevard from 1870-1914, but gradually fell into disrepair, and was no longer sufficient for the population's trading needs. In 1912, the local colonial government decided that it was time to build a new market. The chosen location was some marshy land, since drained, where the market stands today. Construction was completed and the new market opened for business in 1914. At the time, it was christened the New Ben Thanh Market. Over time, the "New" faded away. Ben Thanh Market is now one of the earliest surviving structures in Ho Chi Minh City.

The market endured bombing damage during military conflicts in the 1940s and 1950s. It eventually underwent a post-wartime renovation in 1985, including expansion. Its iconic clock tower is maintained as it had been in the original market and is now a symbol of the city. There is a secret shrine behind the clock tower on the second floor that vendors use to pray for a successful day of selling in the market.

One thing you will notice as you enter the market is the number-based organization scheme. Each vendor has a number for their particular stall. The numbering starts at the South Gate (the gate near the outside traffic circle). From this point, row by row, the numbers increase by one hundred. The stall numbers, although sometimes not entirely sequential, can help you find specific vendors and navigate the scene. The scheme is useful for designating meeting locations. For example, the 1400s are near the North Gate where meat, fish, and fresh produce vendors are located. The section of the market to enjoy breakfast, lunch, or some delicious, colorful Vietnamese coconut "jelly" drinks starts around the 1000s.

If you need a public restroom, one is available in the northeast corner of the market near the end of the 1400s. For more information about the market and how to shop and bargain here, visit the Ben Thanh Market entry under the *Major Sights* section in this book.

After spending some time wandering the aisles and perhaps procuring a souvenir or two, find the 700s row and proceed to the East Gate. If you reach the 800s, you are heading west. Turn around and go back the opposite way. Exit the East Gate (*Cua Dong*) near vendors #741 and #779.

Once outside, carefully cross Phan Boi Chau Street using the crosswalk to your right. If you are new to crossing the busy streets of Ho Chi Minh City, familiarize yourself with the local art of street crossing (see *Getting Around*). In general, motorbikes will tend to bend their route and travel around you as you cross, yet cars and vans arrogantly will not. Your best bet is to wait until things are clear before crossing and watch for speeding motorbikes coming around the corner.

This location on Phan Boi Chau Street (Phan Boi Chau was an early 20th century Vietnamese nationalist and scholar who sought support internationally for gaining independence from France) is where the night market occurs. In the evening, outdoor eateries line up side-by-side and assemble their makeshift charcoal grills for cooking seafood and other traditional Vietnamese dishes. Full dinner service is provided under covered tents. Be sure to come back and visit this night market to experience these culinary delights. While the shopping can be touristy at the night market, there is usually a vibrant local social scene. Hours are nightly from 7 p.m. to midnight.

After you have crossed, turn right and continue down the sidewalk. If you see any fresh coconut juice vendors (you can drink the fresh juice right out of the coconut), or anyone grilling little bananas over a charcoal grill, it is highly suggested that you try either, perhaps after negotiating the price a little. The warm coconut sauce poured over the grilled bananas is total depravity.

On your left as you walk ahead, you will notice a *Pho 24* shop. This shop peddles a fast food version of Vietnam's national dish *pho*. You will see many instances of this franchise around the city and throughout Vietnam. Franchisees are now even setting up shop in other countries, including outside of Asia. The restaurant chain has been purchased multiple times, including in part from local coffee giant Highlands Coffee and a Philippines-based fast food group. Perhaps because of having multiple owners, the chain's quality has suffered somewhat over the years. New owners are attempting to revive it into a globally successful franchise brand and a higher-quality *pho* vendor once again.

When you reach the corner (#2), you will be at the intersection of Phan Boi Chau and Le Loi (*Duong* in the street sign means "street"). A Phuc Long coffee shop is here, another local chain that caters to younger Vietnamese coffee-drinking socializers. With Le Loi Street to your left, look to your right and you will see the energetic traffic circle in front of Ben Thanh Market. Beyond that is the beginning of a long rectangular park. The park was the terminus of the old railroad line that served the city before the track's dismantling. Sometimes the park hosts live concerts. Many major city events, including those held to celebrate the annual Tet (New Year) holiday, occur there. A few blocks beyond in the same direction lies the Pham Ngu Lao backpacker area, as well as Bui Vien Street, known as "foreigner central." There is an abundance of nightlife there to explore on your own later. From this spot, you can also see the bus station across the traffic circle.

From here, turn left on Le Loi Street and begin walking. Le Loi was a famous Vietnamese emperor who led a heroic revolt in the country's independence struggle from China in the 1400s. You will walk past gift shops, coffee shops, art stores, and other vendors as you stroll down Le Loi. This street is a major transportation artery in Ho Chi Minh City. Across the street to your right, you will see a building with the name *Benh Vien Da Khoa*. This is a hospital.

On your left, at address 70 Le Loi, just before you get to Nguyen Trung Truc Street, is a little shop called L'Usine (#3). This is a classic apparel and gift shop opened by expats. It is an example of a modern retail shop with character, an emerging trend in the city. This is one of two locations (the other is on Dong Khoi Street). The ground floor houses the retail store. Upstairs through the back is a pleasant coffee shop with Western lunches, pastries, and fresh juice. There is an outside balcony perch for customers who wish to view the bustling street activity below. There is a restroom on the ground floor. After exiting the store, continue down Le Loi.

Carefully cross Nguyen Trung Tuc Street. If you were to walk half a block to your left down this street, you would find a little sidewalk restaurant called *Xoi Ga Number One*, a great place to try a street food version of *xoi ga*, a local chicken and sticky rice dish (see the street food listing under *Where to Eat* for more information). For now, however, continue straight on Le Loi and then carefully cross Nam Ky Khoi Nghia Street.

On your left at 36 Le Loi, you will see a little alley (#4), called a *hem* in the Vietnamese language. This is Taka Plaza (look for the Ha Ha Sushi sign, with luck still in existence). Down this alley there is the sushi restaurant, a little boutique hotel, a coffee shop, and a rooftop restaurant. There is also a place for locals to park their motorbikes.

There is nothing particularly exceptional about this alley. It is an appropriate place, however, to mention that there are often many little shops, restaurants, and other curiosities to see down these small alleys. These off-street corridors are worth exploring, as they are where some of the city's best finds are hidden. Skipping them would mean missing much that the city has to offer. There is another *hem* later in the tour of more interest.

A little farther along Le Loi is the Sax n' Art Jazz Club at 28 Le Loi (see the *Nightlife* section). Stop here for a moment, as this is an excellent place for a city vantage point. Directly to your right, you can see the recently built boat-sail shaped Bitexco Financial Tower (see *Other Sights* for more information). Straight up Le Loi in the distance, a little to your right (you might need to look through and around a tree) is the Caravelle Hotel and the Sheraton Hotel off Dong Khoi Street that we will get to later on the tour.

Turn left onto Pasteur Street. Note that at busier times, motorbikers may illegally speed down the actual sidewalk here to beat the traffic, so be careful walking (as always in Ho Chi Minh City). To your left as you walk is the Liberty Citypoint Hotel (#5) at 59 Pasteur. It opened in late 2014 with an upscale six-theater modern cinema, including "sweet box" seating available for couples to watch films together. The coffee shop in front is an inviting location to enjoy a *ca phe sua da* (sweetened Vietnamese milk coffee over ice, pronounced "kah fay soo-uh dah") and some riveting people watching. If you are feeling hot, thirsty, or both, purchase a beverage to go in a plastic cup.

Walking up Pasteur (a street named for the famous French chemist and vaccine discoverer), you will pass Chuck's Burgers on the left at 71 Pasteur. Chuck is Vietnamese, but lived in New York and Los Angeles for over thirty years. If during your visit you would like a break from Vietnamese food, his American-style, made-to-order hamburgers are about as appetizing as they come. You can also try local craft beer from the Pasteur Street Brewing Company here.

If you were to continue up Pasteur for four more blocks from this spot, you would pass through the park in front of Reunification Palace, the former South Vietnamese national headquarters (see *Major Sights* for more information). If you were to continue after that, you would enter the city's District 3.

Instead, continue only down to the end of the block. Just past the Starbucks coffee shop across the street, make a right onto Le Thanh Ton Street, named after another famous emperor. Walk twenty yards or so. You will pass the Rex Hotel on your right. We will discuss that famous hotel in a few moments from a different vantage point. For now, we are focusing on the neoclassical city hall building on the left (#6), inspired and modeled after the *Hotel-de-Ville* (city hall) in Paris.

Built in 1908, the colonial structure was renamed the Ho Chi Minh City People's Committee building in 1975 after the end of the Vietnam War. While the building is an active government center and is not open to the public (it is the seat of local government), admiring the architecture of one of Ho Chi Minh City's famous landmarks is an impressive experience. Try to imagine the hanging chandeliers inside.

Continue down Le Thanh Ton Street as you scan the details of the colonial city hall structure. At the clock tower, turn right at the pedestrian park on Nguyen Hue Boulevard. You will see the back of the statue of Ho Chi Minh, the communist leader for which the city is now named after having been called Saigon prior to 1976. Walk towards the statue (#7). This street used to be a major canal. Like many others in the city, it was entirely filled in with dirt for sanitation reasons and to provide more real estate for roads. It recently became pedestrianized and is now a pleasant promenade. This street also becomes the heart of the annual Tet celebrations, when it is transformed into "Flower Street," and is where the holiday crowds gather. In 2016, free 24-hour Wi-Fi was made available on and around Nguyen Hue Boulevard, helpful if you need a quick email check.

When you arrive at the statue, turn around and face Ho Chi Minh with the clock tower of city hall behind him. Viewing city hall from here or farther down Nguyen Hue is especially spectacular at night with the floodlights on. This is worth returning to in the evening to see if you have time to do so.

Who Was Ho Chi Minh?

Ho Chi Minh was the President of the Democratic Republic of Vietnam (North Vietnam) from 1945, when he publicly declared Vietnam's independence after the Second World War, until his death in 1969 at the height of the conflict with the United States and the Republic of Vietnam (South Vietnam). He also served as Prime Minister from 1946-1955. He was the founder of the Indochinese Communist Party. While he never lived to see the unification of Vietnam, he is considered by many to be one of the more influential politicians worldwide of the 20th century.

Ho Chi Minh means "one who is enlightened" in Vietnamese. It is one of over at least a dozen names (and perhaps as many as fifty) either chosen by or given to the man. He was born in 1890 as *Nguyen Sinh Cung* in the village of Kim Lien, Nghe An province, in central Vietnam, a village approximately halfway between Hanoi and the imperial capital city of Hue. His birth province had been the center of resistance during the thousand years of Chinese occupation Vietnam had endured. His father was an anti-colonial nationalist and also a Confucian scholar and teacher, helping Ho Chi Minh to learn Chinese at an early age (much of Ho Chi Minh's later poetry, including poems written in prison and studied by Vietnamese high school students today, were written in Chinese). His mother also came from a local, educated family.

Ho Chi Minh began traveling internationally around age twenty. His journey began in 1911 aboard a French steam ship as a cook where he landed in Europe at the port of Marseilles, France. On arrival, he took odd jobs such as a photo editor and pastry chef and traveled to many different countries, including Germany, Britain, Italy, and presumably the US (it has been difficult for scholars to find evidence of his self-declared stays in New York and Boston).

After moving to Paris in 1917 during the First World War, he became interested in politics, especially socialism and anti-colonialism. In 1919, as his interest and passion in politics grew, he petitioned the US at the Versailles Peace Talks conference for the civil rights of the Vietnamese people under colonial rule. He cited the spirit and language of America's Declaration of Independence, which was a direct appeal to US President Woodrow Wilson. While his requests to the US and other countries were ignored, his speaking out did result in his becoming a soon-to-be-famous symbol of anti-colonialism back in Vietnam. *Nguyen Ai Quoc*, meaning "Nguyen the Patriot" (another name he had given himself), had arrived.

The political peers who did listen and take an interest in Ho Chi Minh and his nation's plight were French communists. As a result of numerous discussions with these opinionated contemporaries, his "radicalization" began and he became a founding member of the French Communist Party in 1920, initiating his long path to power. Three years later in 1923, he first visited Moscow under the passport of a Chinese merchant. There, he became even more deeply involved in communism after becoming acquainted with Leon Trotsky and Joseph Stalin, and intently studying Marxist theory. Because of his travels, Ho Chi Minh was becoming fluent in many languages, including English, French, and Russian in addition to his Vietnamese and Chinese.

He continued to China in 1924 where he remained heavily involved in communist politics and began speaking to young Vietnamese revolutionaries about independence for Vietnam. He was eventually arrested in Hong Kong in 1931 for his revolutionary activities, as part of a crackdown on such actions being enforced by Chiang Kai-Shek, the then nationalist President of China. In Hong Kong, the British, after inaccurately informing the French that Ho Chi Minh had passed away (and perhaps purposely to agitate), released him in 1933. He again traveled back to Russia for an extended period and continued his studies and political activities. He returned to China in 1938 and then in 1941 finally returned to Vietnam. It was then he began to act on his teachings, becoming the leader of a yet unrecognized political faction.

In 1941, Ho Chi Minh helped revive the Viet Minh, then a loose network of communist and socialist sects intent on liberating Vietnam from the French colonialists. He transformed the organization into a single unit during Japan's Second World War occupation of Vietnam. With support and weapons provided by the United States and China, Japan's enemies, the Viet Minh fought against the Japanese. With Japan's surrender to the United States in 1945, Ho Chi Minh declared Vietnam's independence with a public speech and his organization turned its efforts to completely removing Vietnam from any type of French control. After years of guerilla warfare, in 1954 the North Vietnamese at last defeated the French colonialists at Dien Bien Phu, effectively ending France's colonialization of Vietnam.

Subsequent to the defeat of the French at Dien Bien Phu, the Geneva Peace Accords were held. In exchange for the exit of French troops from Vietnam, a line was drawn temporarily dividing Vietnam into the North and the South at the 17th parallel to reflect post-colonial military, nationalistic, and geographical divisions. President Ho Chi Minh relocated the capital of his political movement to Hanoi and began efforts to unite the entire country under communist rule. While the headquarters of the newly formed Democratic Republic of Vietnam (North Vietnam) were the President's Palace in Hanoi, Ho Chi Minh is said to have lived in the stilted house out back, rather than the palace itself, choosing a simpler day-to-day existence.

Ho Chi Minh's unification efforts were strongly opposed by South Vietnam and its leader Ngo Dinh Diem, who was vehemently anti-communist and had a powerful ally in the United States. The US supported South Vietnam in an attempt to prevent the so-called "domino effect" of Asian countries falling one-by-one under the rule and influence of globally spreading communism. This conflict eventually led to the Vietnam War, where local skirmishes escalated into one of the major conflicts of the 20th century, causing the deaths of over two million Vietnamese and 58,000 US servicemen.

Ho Chi Minh died in 1969 from heart failure during the height of the conflict. This was a year after the Tet Offensive in 1968, deemed by many to be a significant psychological blow to the ant-communist forces politically—and the turning point of the war. Towards the end of his life, Ho Chi Minh became primarily a symbol of his country's struggle for independence and unification, and the Vietnamese affectionately called him "Uncle Ho." Up until the end, he staunchly insisted that "all non-Vietnamese must forever leave Vietnam."

In 1976, a year after the Fall of Saigon and the unification of Vietnam, the communist government renamed Saigon to Ho Chi Minh City in his honor.

Today, many Vietnamese revere Ho Chi Minh for bringing independence to Vietnam from the last of its subjugators. His body can still be publicly viewed at his tomb in Hanoi. All of Vietnam's currency notes also commemorate Ho Chi Minh. But, as with many world leaders, opinions can vary on any one individual. Many former South Vietnamese in enclaves around the world still denounce Ho Chi Minh and his actions and do not support the current government. Over time, these differences and continued hostilities may continue to fade. Many former South Vietnamese have now peacefully returned to Vietnam, relegating the tragic war to the ash heap of history. The wounds of the past will likely one day completely heal. Vietnam and its people will hopefully move forward in unison, and the vision of a truly unified Vietnam will be realized.

Now, look up high to your left to the roof balcony of the famous Vietnam War-era Rex Hotel. This rooftop bar was a place where officers and journalists fraternized during the war, often watching flashes and hearing explosions in the distance while they sipped their cocktails. It was the location of the daily news conference from the American military command known by many as the "Five O'clock Follies," as journalists suspected that neither complete nor accurate information was being provided from the commanding generals at these press conferences. There was a large degree of cynicism over the positive outlook conveyed by some of the military leaders, hence the humorous name. The balcony these days is a befitting location for a few early-evening rooftop beverages to enjoy views of the city overlooking Nguyen Hue Boulevard, and also to reflect upon the city's wartime past.

If you were to continue down Nguyen Hue Boulevard behind you from this spot in front of the statue, you would walk through the heart of Ho Chi Minh City's commercial district. You would pass the iconic Bitexco Financial Tower on your right, and eventually end up down by the Saigon River.

Instead, walk back towards the city hall clock tower and turn right on Le Thanh Ton Street. Continue down Le Thanh Ton Street.

The Union Square shopping complex (#8) is on the right as you pass. You will find many high-end shops representative of the kind of luxury shopping that is proliferating throughout the city, especially in District 1. Ralph Lauren, Hugo Boss, Versace, Nike, and Brooks Brothers are all present. This is a stark contrast to the hectic, bargain-seeking, local shopping experience found at Ben Thanh Market. Vietnam Airlines has a large, comfortable ticket office on the second floor of the Union Square shopping complex, ideal for exploring and building travel itineraries in Vietnam and throughout Southeast Asia with the help of airline representatives.

Continue farther down Le Thanh Ton Street. At the end of city hall, turn left onto famous Dong Khoi Street (more about this street later). Next, walk up half a block and face the modern Asian architecture twin-towered Vincom Center (#9) on your right. Vincom Center is another shopping complex. It has a sprawling underground

Pan-Asian food court complex (see *Where to Eat* for additional information) to serve hungry shoppers.

Stand directly across from the word "Center" on the Vincom Center building. Then, look up to your left at ten o'clock using the clock position analogy. You will see a little square platform (#10) on top of the building. A tree might block your view, in which case you might need to shuffle a little to the left or right.

This platform was the site of the famous helicopter rescue during the fall of Saigon in 1975. The event was immortalized in several evocative photographs taken at the time.

A CIA employee helps Vietnamese evacuees onto an Air America helicopter from the top of 22 Gia Long Street (Bettman/Getty Images)

This famous address at 22 Gia Long Street (now 22 Ly Tu Trong, as many street names changed after 1975 when the new ruling regime took over) was actually an apartment used by the CIA. The people in the photograph were escaping through the roof. The predetermined evacuation signal had been given over the radio. The words "It's 105 degrees and rising," followed by thirty seconds of Bing Crosby's *I'm Dreaming of a White Christmas* were broadcast live on the airwaves, signaling total evacuation of the city as the North Vietnamese converged on a helpless, unfortified Saigon. Clearly, of these South Vietnamese citizens who worked for the US government, only twelve to fourteen people were likely able to board this particular helicopter. The remaining individuals waited for more helicopters to arrive, but unfortunately, this was the only one that departed from this location during the total evacuation. Many have mistakenly thought this photograph to be a picture of the helicopter escapes at the American Embassy (of which there were a large number).

Continue farther up Dong Khoi Street. You will next cross Ly Tu Trong Street. If you were to turn left, the socially conscious Huong Lai restaurant (described in the *Where to Eat* section) is at #38 Ly Tu Trong. The former US Embassy, now an American consulate, is a couple of blocks to the right. There was much street combat near the embassy during the Vietnam War, especially during the Tet Offensive in 1968.

After carefully crossing Ly Tu Trong Street, continue up Dong Khoi until you arrive at the bottom of Paris Commune Square (it was named John F. Kennedy Square until 1975). This is where the *Notre Dame Cathedral Basilica* stands. The best way to get to the basilica (Pope John XXIII gave it "basilica" status in a 1962 ceremony) is to turn left at Nguyen Du Street, and then turn right to follow the crosswalk in front of the *Coffee Bean and Tea Leaf* coffee shop (an optimal location for an afternoon coffee with a view). Take a right again at the crosswalk crossing Cong Xa Paris Street and then stand in front of and facing the statue of *Mary* (#11).

In 1959, the *Our Lady of Peace* granite statue was ordered from Rome while a local Vietnamese bishop was visiting the Vatican. The statue arrived the same year and was placed in front of the church. Upon its blessing, including a prayer for *Our Lady*, the church was henceforth known as Notre Dame Cathedral (*Notre Dame* translates to "Our Lady" in French).

In October of 2005, a well-known incident occurred when this same statue was purported to have shed tears down the right cheek of its face. This brought a great deal of commotion and halted traffic as onlookers attempted to witness these supposed tears, attracting thousands of locals and tourists.

Notre Dame Cathedral Basilica, officially named *Our Lady of the Immaculate Conception*, is a neo-Romanesque style church (see the rounded arches inside indicating this style) made of red brick situated on Paris Commune Square. [Note: Currently, the interior of Notre Dame is closed for renovation until 2020.] It is considered neo-Romanesque because it was built in a revival-style inspired by and according to Romanesque church architecture. This style was prevalent in the Middle Ages, primarily in the 10th, 11th, and 12th centuries, before Gothic architecture got its footing. The Roman

Catholic Church built this cathedral for French colonialists who needed a larger church for worship, rather than the pagoda on Ngo Duc Ke Street (that structure had been too small to accommodate a growing congregation).

All the building materials for the construction of the church were imported from France, including the red bricks that originated in Marseilles. These bricks still maintain their reddish color today. The colorful stained-glass windows were produced in Chartres Province, France, an area famous for its medieval stain glass production. The first stone of the structure was placed in 1877. The cathedral was officially finished and then ceremonially dedicated and blessed during Easter Sunday mass in 1880. Its original name was the *State Cathedral*.

Two bell towers were added in 1895, each with six bronze bells. The height of the cathedral from the ground to the top of the added cross is 60.5 meters.

While not as grand as some of its European counterparts, it is unusual architecture for Vietnam. It is a beautiful, sacred, and staunch reminder of the country's romantic, though often oppressive, French-controlled colonial past.

If the church is open, go inside. Men, if you don't take your hat off, a charismatic child may come over to politely remind you to do so.

On both sides of the entrance, you will see a series of "thank you" plaques placed for the previous benefactors of the church. Take a little while to view the nave and its Romanesque arches. Try to imagine a colonial mass occurring over a hundred years ago (without air conditioning).

As you exit the church, turn to your left. You will see the French colonial architecture of the main post office with both Baroque and neo-Baroque design components. The building was recently painted a somewhat uninviting mustard color. Despite this, it is one of the grander examples of French colonial architecture in all of Vietnam.

Facing the post office, carefully cross the street at the crosswalk. Walk towards the post office and enter the building (#12). Inside there is a large portrait of Ho Chi Minh. There are also two large maps on the walls of appreciable interest, including one from 1936 showing telegraphic lines between various locations in Vietnam and also Cambodia (shown as *Cambodge* in French). The other is a regional map from 1892 showing Saigon and its surrounding area.

You can buy postcards and gifts, send mail, and use ATMs that are inside the old converted phone booths.

When you exit, turn left and head down Dong Khoi Street back the way you came before arriving at the Cathedral. As you cross Nguyen Du Street to return to Dong Khoi, note that down to your left is both a Mobifone store and a Vinaphone store where you can obtain a local sim card for your smartphone or other mobile device. Continue on back down Dong Khoi.

Now that we are at the top of Dong Khoi Street, it is an appropriate time to provide some historical context to the most famous street in Ho Chi Minh City. Originally, the street was named Sixth Street. Early on at the city's inception, the streets in Saigon were given ordinal numbers as names. In 1865, French Commander De La Grandiere renamed Sixth Street as Rue Catinat after a French warship. Rue Catinat became the major thoroughfare of street life in colonial Saigon with all the scintillating European hustle and bustle of the day focused here. It also boasted much of the great French colonial architecture in the city, some of which you will see as we stroll along.

After the Second World War, the South Vietnamese renamed the street *Tu Do* Street ("Liberty Street" after the end of Japanese occupation). Tu Do became the center of US military fraternizing, with several soldier bars known for some risqué nightlife (some vestiges remain). In 1975, after the communists took over, the street again was renamed *Dong Khoi*, meaning "Total Revolution" in Vietnamese. This name remains today, and the street still runs through the soul of downtown Ho Chi Minh City.

Continue back past Vincom Center and also past the Parkson Shopping Complex on your left. You will then arrive at the venerable, grand Continental Hotel (#13). Turn left just past the Continental and just before the Opera House onto Lam Son Square (named Place Garnier under the French). This will put you in front of the Continental Hotel. The Opera House is across the street, but we will get to that later.

The Hotel Continental was the grandest hotel in all of Saigon and perhaps the best-known landmark in all of French colonial *Cochinchina* (what the French called the southern third of Vietnam). Many scenes from Graham Greene's *The Quiet American* novel took place here at this hotel and its terrace. Throughout its history it has been frequented by upscale business travelers, journalists, and political crowds, but these days mostly accommodates tourists. During the Vietnam War, the hotel served as host to contingents from both Time and Newsweek as both magazines had their news bureaus here. Saigon Tourist, a state-owned travel and tourist enterprise, now owns the hotel.

Continue on the sidewalk past the Continental Hotel. Behind the Opera House on your right is Highlands Coffee, part of the Vietnamese chain of coffee locations. If you need a break, stop in, as an iced Vietnamese coffee and a slice of *banh chuoi* (banana cake) might hit the spot right about now.

As you move along on Lam Son Square, on your left you will pass the beautiful modern and recently renovated (in 2015) Park Hyatt hotel that has been built in a French colonial, albeit modern style. If you look inside, there is a piano lounge just off to the right of the entrance serving refreshing (and expensive) drinks and snacks for an afternoon break in elegant comfort. The hotel is on the site of the old Brinks Hotel, which housed American officers during the Vietnam War. The Brinks Hotel was car-bombed in 1964, killing two Americans and injuring sixty others. Continue walking past the front of the hotel until you reach Hai Ba Trung Street. Look to your left in front of the hotel for the bombing memorial that commemorates the tragic event (#14).

Next, cross Hai Ba Trung Street at the crosswalk. Turn left, and at approximately one hundred yards to your right (just before the El Gaucho Steakhouse at 74 Hai Bai Trung), you will see an open entrance, presumably with a makeshift sign above it displaying the words "The Courtyard."

This is the entrance to the Old Opium Refinery (#15). In 1881, during the prosperous "golden age" of opium, the French built the refinery as *La Manufacture d'Opium*. By the early 1900s, opium production was one of the higher sources of income for French colonial officers. Most of the opium processed here was grown in and imported from India. Today, there are several restaurants here, most of which offer international cuisine. There is the recommended Hoa Tuc restaurant (see *Where to Eat*), providing well-presented traditional and contemporary Vietnamese dishes with the excellent Vietnamese cooking school on its second floor (see *Tours and*

Activities). This is a pleasant courtyard to visit for a lovely dinner in the evenings.

After a look around, leave the courtyard the way you came in. From here, we are going to head back past the Opera House towards Dong Khoi Street, but this time on the opposite side of Lam Son Square. After leaving the courtyard of the Opium Refinery, turn left and walk again approximately one hundred yards. Cross Cao Ba Quat Street and then the adjacent Nguyen Sieu Street. Turn right and cross Hai Ba Trung Street again until you are back on Lam Son Square (there is a parking lot on your right within the square).

Continue along Lam Son Square, passing some model ship stores (including traditional Chinese *junk* boat models). You will see a handful of restaurants on your left. The Highlands Coffee shop is on your right along with the Opera House. Keep walking until you reach the Caravelle Hotel up ahead on the left.

The Caravelle Hotel (#16) was opened in 1959. It has an extensive wartime legacy. The hotel comprises two structures. The original structure is closer to Dong Khoi Street and is only nine stories high. The second taller tower was later added. The famous Saigon Saigon Bar on the ninth floor of the older structure was a famous watering hole for foreign journalists during the Vietnam War. Correspondents would watch the war unfold on the outskirts of the city from the rooftop, which now provides a great view of Dong Khoi and the rest of the city. A bomb targeting foreign journalists exploded here in 1964. Fortunately, there were no fatalities as a result of the blast. It was also presumably the location of several meetings held in secret by military leaders that were critical of South Vietnam President Ngo Dinh Diem prior to the coup in which he was overthrown and then assassinated. It was the home of the Australian and New Zealand embassies and was the headquarters of television news outlets NBC, ABC, and CBS during the war. In the evenings, there is usually some delightful, relaxing, jazz-like lounge singing occurring in the lobby to enjoy. The rooftop bar still provides nightly musical entertainment as well.

After exiting the hotel, continue on towards Dong Khoi Street where we will take a closer look at the opera complex. Turn right on Dong Khoi Street and walk over to the front of the Opera House (#17) and face it.

The Opera House opened to performances in 1897 with eight hundred seats and became the center of life for French colonialists. Like its counterpart in Hanoi, the design was inspired by the venerable Palace Garnier in Paris. Originally, because of the intense heat in the city, the theater was only open for four months a year from October to January.

In 1944, the Opera House was damaged during Allied bombing attacks against the Japanese. In 1954, it was used as a shelter for French colonial citizens after the Viet Minh defeated the French at Dien Bien Phu. From 1956-1975, the building was used as the lower house of the South Vietnamese Assembly. In 1975, after the Vietnam War, it became a theater once again, although this time with a communist kitschy look and feel. It was restored and renovated in 1998 and today is used for conferences and various live shows and theater. It is open to the public only during events and performances. Depending on the show, tickets generally range from $25-$75 USD. You can see from the posters in front of the Opera House what events are playing on a given date. For ticket information, see the Opera House section under the *Major Sights* section of this book.

Cross back from the Opera House on Dong Khoi Street again from where you just came. Pass the Caravelle Hotel on your left and continue on. As you walk, you will pass the Sheraton Hotel (#18). If you would like to catch a glimpse inside the mighty Sheraton, then turn left on Dong Du Street and walk a hundred feet to do so and then return to this point. Otherwise, continue along on Dong Khoi Street.

You will shortly reach Mac Thi Buoi Street. Mac Thi Buoi was a famous female revolutionary guerilla fighting for independence from France. Turn right on Mac Thi Buoi. A few yards on your right will be the recommended Tan Hoang Long Hotel (see *Where to Sleep*), a well-positioned, inexpensive mini-hotel. A few doors beyond that is the Ru'nam Cafe, a classic, cozy spot for an afternoon snack, a traditional Vietnamese coffee, and an offering of local desserts.

On your left is an alley (*hem* again in Vietnamese) labeled address 71. Walk down this clandestine alley (#19 on the map). This is another example of a hidden *hem* in Ho Chi Minh City that upon entry reveals an enticing collection of establishments. Down this alley is the recommended and pleasingly decorated Quan An Vietnamese

Bistro. There is also a Thai restaurant, the recommended Nguoi Sai Gon coffee shop and lounge-singing venue, and a couple of other restaurants.

Leave the alley after looking around and turn back right on Mac Thi Buoi. Then, make another right to continue walking down Dong Khoi Street. On the left side of the street is Khanhcasa Tea House, another comfortable stop for some coffee and conversation in a plush environment. Just past that is the Moo Steakhouse, a recent steak and wine establishment with the stylish outdoor Flex night club above it.

On your right is the Long Bar, Times Square, and the Reverie Hotel complex (#20). The newly established Long Bar is billed as a city-block-long bar (actually it is several connected bars nearly fifty yards long in aggregate). The new Reverie Hotel Saigon, opened in 2015, is currently the swankiest and highest-priced accommodations option in Ho Chi Minh City. The world-class hotel with an Italian interior design style occupies the top floors of the thirty-nine-story Times Square building.

A little farther up on your left on Dong Khoi Street is the Grand Hotel Saigon. Built in 1930 with chandeliered, classical elegance, it has a rooftop bar with live, nightly piano music.

Moving along Dong Khoi, on your right are the Maxim establishments. First is Maxim's Restaurant. Beyond that is Maxim's Music Club, a classic "Old Saigon" live music ballroom dancing bar and club that has had this address since 1925. It was reopened in 2012 with Vietnamese and international musicians providing the backdrop for the waltz and the rumba. An expensive cocktail and spirits menu caters to a dressy, classy, older clientele who romantically swing and sway to the intimate rhythms of the band throughout the evening.

Finally, on your right is the world-renowned Majestic Hotel (#21). Japanese Imperial Forces occupied this grand location during the Second World War. Its rooftop bar was a favorite of author Graham Greene and his fictional Thomas Fowler character in the novel *The Quiet American*, likely because of the views of the Saigon River and the cool evening breezes the river produces. Other luminaries to stay here include W. Somerset Maugham, French actress Catherine Deneuve (who had a starring role in the movie *Indochine*), and multiple foreign presidents and prime ministers. It is well-known that French colonial agents often met with spies at this hotel early in the 20th century. It was also a point of spy rendezvous during the Vietnam War. Grenade grills covered the windows of the Vietnamese Cyclo Restaurant within the hotel during the Vietnam War to protect diners.

That's a wrap for the walking tour. You can now enjoy a refreshing drink on the rooftop of the Majestic Hotel, swing back up Dong Khoi and cool off with some drinks in one of the myriad establishments that were discovered on the tour, grab local transportation and return to your place of local residence, or commence whatever your next Ho Chi Minh City experience might be.

Major Sights

Reunification Palace
(**www.dinhdoclap.gov.vn**) (135 Nam Ky Khoi Nghia Street, District 1)
07:30 – 11:00, 13:00 – 16:00, daily, adults: 30,000 VND

Also known as Independence Palace, this complex was the presidential palace for the Republic of South Vietnam, serving as the office and official residence of South Vietnam's president during its existence. It is now memorialized as the location where the Vietnam War officially ended on April 30th, 1975, when North Vietnamese soldiers in Soviet-made T-54 tanks bulldozed through the front gates. A North Vietnamese soldier famously waved the flag of the victors from the balcony of the building. This event signified the tragic end of the Republic of South Vietnam and its surrender was announced that afternoon. Acting President Duong Van Minh (in office for only two days, although he had previously served as president in 1963 for three months after the assassination of President Ngo Dinh Diem) was taken prisoner after officially announcing the dissolution of the Saigon government over the radio. This completed the total communist victory across the entire country.

A visit to this former residence and office is a haunting trip through time. The hallways, meeting rooms, reception rooms, and underground bunkers have changed little since that day. The entire complex has been preserved as a museum, enabling visitors to acquire a sense of what the confines of the building were like before and during the Vietnam War.

Reunification Palace, the former headquarters of South Vietnam

A colonial residence was the original structure built on this site. Then, in 1873 the Norodom Palace (named after the King of Cambodia) was built here. It became the French Governor's Palace for governing Cochinchina for fourteen years until the French moved the seat of colonial government to Hanoi. The original grand palace was built in French Second Empire style and housed several colonial governors.

During the Second World War, Japan took over the palace and it became the headquarters of Japanese military officials during Japan's occupation of Saigon. It was returned to France at the end of the war after the Japanese surrender to the Allies.

The palace was then handed over to South Vietnamese President Ngo Dinh Diem in 1954 after the defeat of the French at Dien Bien Phu and the partitioning of Vietnam at the 17th parallel into North Vietnam and South Vietnam in accordance with the outcome of the Geneva Conference held that year.

In 1962, renegade South Vietnamese pilots opposed to President Diem bombed the palace in an attempted coup, destroying the entire left wing. This resulted in a decision to rebuild the entire structure.

Diem commissioned and rebuilt the new Independence Palace, which would later become Reunification Palace. Its grand opening was in 1967. From high above, one can see that the building is shaped like the Chinese character *Ji*, which means "good luck." Diem, assassinated in 1963, was never able to see its completion or live in the new palace.

Nguyen Van Thieu, President of South Vietnam from 1967 to 1975, used the presidential palace only for official duties. A colonial mansion a few blocks away at 161 Pasteur served as his private residence.

Since the end of the war, the palace has been used for historic events such as the signing of the US-Vietnam bilateral agreement that included Vietnam's entry into the World Trade Organization in 2007. Today, you can visit the president's office, war rooms, banquet rooms, cabinet rooms, state rooms, living quarters, the library, conference halls, reception areas, waiting areas, and much more. The war rooms, the central nervous system of the South Vietnamese war effort, are impressive to visit with their large maps and various communications equipment, as are the various underground bomb tunnels.

Dining room of Reunification Palace

Notre Dame Cathedral Basilica
(East end of Dong Khoi Street, District 1)
08:00 – 11:00, 15:00 – 17:00, closed Sundays for worship (tourists can attend), free

[Note: Currently, the interior of Notre Dame is closed for renovation until 2020.] Notre Dame Basilica, officially named Our Lady of the Immaculate Conception, is a neo-Romanesque style church made of red brick that sits on Paris Commune Square in the heart of the city. This iconic landmark, the largest Christian structure in the city, is next to the colonial-style Central Post Office at the east end of Dong Khoi Street (the opposite end from the Saigon River). It is acknowledged as *neo*-Romanesque because it was built in a revival style inspired by the existing Romanesque cathedral architecture once prevalent in the Middle Ages—primarily in the 10th, 11th, and 12th centuries—before Gothic architecture got its footing. Another clue is the interior nave with its rounded arches.

View of Notre Dame Basilica and surrounding area (Thoai/Shutterstock.com)

The Roman Catholic Church built this cathedral for French colonialists who needed a larger church for worship than the pagoda on Ngo Duc Ke Street, which had been determined to be too small for a growing congregation. While not as grand as some of its European counterparts, the cathedral represents unique architecture for Vietnam. Inspired by and based on Notre Dame Cathedral in Paris, it is a beautiful, sacred, and staunch reminder of Vietnam's colonial, if not at times romantic yet brutal, French-controlled past.

Construction on the first church at this location occurred from 1863-1865. It had been named Saigon Church and was built entirely out of wood. Unfortunately, termites severely damaged this original structure. It was then determined that a larger, grander church would be built out of a more long-lasting material for use by generations to come.

All building materials for this new construction, based on a winning design from eighteen separate submissions, were imported from France, including the red bricks that originated in Marseilles. The colorful stained-glass windows, each of which depicted a scene from the Bible, were produced in Chartres Province, France. The first stone of the cathedral was placed in 1877, and the cathedral was officially finished and then ceremonially dedicated and blessed during Easter Sunday mass in 1880. Its original name was the State Cathedral.

Two bell towers were added in 1895, each with six bronze bells. The height of the cathedral from the ground to the top of the added cross is 60.5 meters.

In 1959, the Our Lady of Peace granite statue was ordered from Rome while a local Vietnamese bishop was visiting the Vatican. The statue arrived the same year and was placed in front of the church. Upon its blessing, including a prayer for *Our Lady*, the church was henceforth known as Notre Dame Cathedral.

In October of 2005, a well-known incident occurred when this same statue was purported to have shed tears down the right cheek of its face, bringing a great deal of commotion and halting traffic as onlookers attempted to witness these supposed tears.

Today, the brick still maintains its reddish color. Some of the original carved tiles have been replaced with those made in Ho Chi Minh City because of bomb damage during the Second World War. The church is now a favorite with local newlyweds for photos.

On both sides of the entrance of the church, you will see a series of "thank you" plaques placed for previous benefactors of the building. Inside, you can see the interior nave and its Romanesque arches. There is an organ with more than seven thousand pipes whose operation is now fully computerized. There are fourteen stations of the cross to view along a walkway, including through the back ambulatory, enabling you to visit the stations sequentially as you move around the cathedral. Several of the side chapels where these stations are located are dedicated to various saints. There is a shrine in honor of Vietnamese Roman Catholic martyrs that were canonized here by Pope John Paul II in 1988.

It is estimated that over six million Vietnamese are Catholics today. Services are given on Sundays in both Vietnamese and English.

Ben Thanh Market

(Phan Boi Chau at Le Loi, District 1)
06:00 – 18:00, daily, free

Ben Thanh Market is a thriving, semi-outdoor, covered, colorful marketplace near downtown Ho Chi Minh City with a long history. Over a thousand vendors here sell fresh produce, meats, seafood, souvenirs, exotic food items, coffee, unique beverages, locally made traditional and modern apparel, and much more, and have been doing so for more than a century. Wide-eyed, fascinated tourists from all over the world wander the stalls and haggle for deals (usually compassionately). It can be difficult to walk through the variety of merchandise without engaging in a potential transaction.

Aerial view of Ben Thanh Market (xuanhuongho/Shutterstock.com)

This market is the center of energy in Ho Chi Minh City. The buying and selling sprawls well beyond the marketplace into adjacent city blocks. The main market complex itself, however, is the heartbeat of the vast network of neighborhood commerce. This is where the action is.

It is not the cheapest place in the city to find souvenirs and local cuisine, nor is it the largest commercial center in town. Still, the diversity of items, the opportunity to deal and converse with locals, and the grand spectacle of it all have made Ben Thanh Market one of the more popular spots in Southeast Asia to participate in the street market game.

At twilight, the streets surrounding Ben Thanh Market turn into an evening flurry of vendors and makeshift restaurants, where the scent of smoking, orange-glowing charcoal reveals grilled seafood that blisters and crackles, while steaming pots of broth bubble away in to the black of night. All of this keeps the market bustling from early in the morning until late in the evening.

Ho Chi Minh City's original markets were established by the Saigon River, not far from here, in the 17th century. Soon after taking control of the city in 1859, the French established a covered market a few blocks from the market's present location on Ham Nghi Street towards the river. The French called this first marketplace *Les Halles Centrales*. Locals began calling it Ben Thanh Market (*Cho Ben Thanh*) because it was a market (*cho*), and it was close to a wharf (*ben*) and the original Gia Dinh Citadel (*thanh*). A blazing fire destroyed it in 1869.

A second "temporary" market existed over on Nguyen Hue Boulevard from 1870-1914. In 1912, it was decided that it was time to build a new permanent market to support the burgeoning local commerce. It was built on some marshy land, since drained, where it stands today and was completed and opened for business in 1914. At the time, it was christened the New Ben Thanh Market. Gradually over time, the "New" faded away. It is now one of the earliest surviving structures in Ho Chi Minh City.

The market endured bombing in the 1940s and 1950s, and underwent a renovation in 1985 to expand and update the complex. Its famous clock tower was maintained as it was in the original market and is now a symbol of the city. There is a secret shrine behind the iconic clock tower on the second floor that vendors use to pray for a successful day in the market.

Visiting the market today is an exhilarating experience. Mornings are best, as the early hour helps for escaping the heat. This is when the seafood and meat markets are at their most frenetic. It is a good idea to pay close attention to your belongings here, as it is a place of tourist congregation.

The market is laid out using a number-based organization scheme, with each vendor having a number for their particular stall. The numbering starts at the South Gate (the gate near the outside traffic circle). Row by row (although sometimes not exactly sequentially) the numbers increase by one hundred as you move through the diverse offerings of goods. The stall numbers can help in finding specific vendors, navigating the market, and perhaps meeting others at a pre-determined location. On the opposite end, near the North Gate where the meat, fish, fresh fruit, and vegetable vendors are, the numbers get into the 1400s. The area of the market to eat breakfast or lunch, or enjoy some tantalizing Vietnamese coconut "jelly" drinks and other colorful beverages, starts around the 1000s.

If you need a public restroom, one is available in the northeast corner of the market near the end of the 1400s.

In the fresh food area in the 1400s, you will find for sale many varieties of Mekong River freshwater fish such as elephant fish, many types of saltwater fish plucked from the sea, dried seafood, snakes and frogs. There is also beef, every imaginable pig part, offal, and a wide selection of fresh poultry. There are vendors selling a variety of fruits and vegetables, dried noodles, spices, chili peppers, and there are even a handful of vegan stalls. You can also find many vendors selling famous varieties of Vietnamese coffee, including the pseudo-"weasel" coffee, a knockoff of the colonial original and another vestige of the city's past.

Because of the volume of traffic and frequent health inspections, food here is some of the freshest in the city. See the *Cuisine of Ho Chi Minh City* section to learn more about Vietnamese ingredients, many of which can be purchased here. Also, several cooking schools, including the Saigon Cooking Class offered at the Hoa Tuc restaurant and listed under *Tours and Activities*, start their instruction with a trip to Ben Thanh Market first thing in the morning to obtain the raw cooking ingredients to be used in class.

In addition to the fresh culinary market, there are many food vendor stalls near the center of the market in the 700s selling prepared, ready-to-eat traditional Vietnamese dishes. These can often be great choices for lunch, as many recognize these versions of Vietnam's famous dishes and soups served here as some of the best in the city. You will find noodle dishes, *goi cuon* (popular Vietnamese lettuce and shrimp rolls), hot and spicy soups such as *pho, bun rieu* and *bun bo Hue*; *banh uot*, and many more traditional dishes. There is an enticing selection of desserts such as an assortment of sweet soups, warm banana desserts, sticky rice, and coconut-based dessert drinks. You might notice, especially at the night market, lots of sticky rice available in a multitude of colors. This is achieved using both artificial and other coloring, as the color of the rice itself is not natural.

From an apparel and appearance standpoint, you can find traditional Vietnamese clothing such as the famous *ao dai* dress, t-shirts, shoes, handbags, hair accessories and products, cosmetics, and jewelry. Souvenirs include chopsticks, handicrafts, art, dishware, and many Vietnamese-made toys and trinkets. Since many of the Vietnamese believe the first customer of the day sets the tone for the day's business, you may snag some bargains early on, but only if you are friendly and don't bargain too hard. Unfriendly, hard-bargaining customers are not an attractive way to set the tone for the day for the vendors either. You will likely not get very far with an overbearing approach.

Other markets (including a larger one in the Chinese District 5 area of Cholon) can be significantly cheaper than Ben Thanh Market. Many entrepreneurs buy at the cheaper markets around the city and then come here to resell to tourists at a higher price. Still, you will find the highest number of English-speaking vendors and obtain the consummate Vietnamese market hall experience here at this centrally located market. Shrewd bargainers may even score a good deal or two. Note that some vendors have signs claiming a "fixed price," which they may or may not budge from. Again, be aware that this area can be a haven for pickpockets and drive-by motorbike purse snatchers. As with all of Ho Chi Minh City, be vigilant.

Temples

There are many interesting, evocative temples throughout Ho Chi Minh City. Most of the temples in town are Buddhist temples. The majority of these temples, many of which were built relatively recently, reflect a practice of Buddhism that is descended from and related to Chinese Buddhism that first appeared in Vietnam nearly two thousand years ago. Visiting at least two or three of these temples is a worthwhile experience if you have the time to do so. Here are some of the more well-known ones:

Jade Emperor Pagoda
(73 Mai Thi Luu Street, District 1)
07:00 – 18:00, daily, free

The Jade Emperor Pagoda, hidden away down a narrow street, is a Taoist temple built by the Chinese in 1909. Taoism is a philosophical religion based on writings in the 6th century BC by the philosopher Lao-Tzu. These writings are known as *the truth*, i.e. the

Tao, which according to Taoists is the force behind everything that exists.

Emperor shrine inside the Jade Pagoda (Frank Fischbach/Shutterstock.com)

This pagoda is also known as the "tortoise" pagoda. It is perhaps the most visually spectacular of the pagodas in Ho Chi Minh City with its wood carvings, statues, various Taoist characters, and incense-filled chambers. There is a small pond outside that is the home of the many tortoises that have given the pagoda its colloquial name.

The Jade Emperor, known as the "god of the heavens," is the primary figure inside. Other statues include the "goddess of fertility" and the "king of hell," who receives all those the Jade Emperor rejects.

Quan Am Pagoda
(12 Lao Tu, District 5)
08:00 – 17:00, daily, free

The Quan Am Pagoda is a Buddhist temple located in Cholon, District 5. Built in the 1800s, it is the oldest in Ho Chi Minh City. It is named for the Vietnamese "goddess of mercy." According to believers she will help anyone in trouble. One summons her simply by calling out her name. Though the pagoda is dedicated to her, there are several other deities present.

The pagoda's ridged roof and colorful figurines depicting life in Cholon are intriguing. There is a large painting and devotion to *Our Lady of the Sea*, demonstrating that the temple was built by maritime communities whose livelihood depended on a seafaring lifestyle. Most of the inscriptions are written in Chinese characters.

The pagoda is active and popular today; however, it is unlikely you will see any working monks. Incense lit here for relatives might burn for a week. The goddess Quan Am is also worshipped in other forms throughout Asia.

The pagoda is approximately twenty minutes by hired car from District 1. If there is interest in visiting, it might be best combined with other attractions in District 5 or nearby District 6, such as Binh Tay Market.

Xa Loi Pagoda

(**www.chuaxaloi.vn**) (89 Ba Huyen Thanh Quan Street, District 3)
07:00 – 11:00, 14:00 – 17:00, daily, free

The Xa Loi Pagoda, located in District 3 and built in 1956, is the largest in Ho Chi Minh City. With its seven stories, it is also the highest in Vietnam. Within the shrine, there is a giant statue of Gautama Buddha (the supreme Buddha of Indian Buddhist origin).

The pagoda served as the headquarters for the Buddhists of South Vietnam prior to the Vietnam War. South Vietnamese troops were accused of vandalizing it in 1963. South Vietnamese President Ngo Dinh Diem was Catholic and characterized by many as hostile to Buddhists. Buddhists protested Diem's hostility, and these protests in turn instigated the raid and vandalism. These acts were a precursor to the self-immolation protest of monk Thich Quang Duc in 1963 on Nguyen Dinh Chieu Street, a five-minute walk from here, where there is a memorial to the event. Xa Loi Pagoda has become a symbol of resistance against the Diem regime.

Mariamman Hindu Temple
(45 Truong Dinh, District 1)
07:30 – 19:00, daily, free

This temple, located in District 1 only a few blocks away from Ben Thanh Market, was built in the 1800s and dedicated to the Hindu goddess Mariamman. There are various statues to the goddess around the outside of the temple. The temple was built by Tamil immigrants from French colonial holdings in South India. They were brought to Vietnam to help build infrastructure during Vietnam's colonial period.

Other Sights

Cu Chi Tunnels
(Ben Dinh & Ben Duoc)
07:00 – 18:00, daily, adults: 100,000 VND + transportation costs

The Cu Chi Tunnels, located about an hour outside of the city center of Ho Chi Minh City, are part of a network of underground passageways used by Viet Cong guerrillas during the Vietnam War. The full network runs underneath much of the entire country. It was built in the late 1940s for resistance purposes during the French reoccupation period after Japanese withdrawal post-Second World War. This tunnel network was significantly expanded during the Vietnam War to aid the North Vietnamese in its takeover of South Vietnam, enabling the communists to move supplies and otherwise outmaneuver American and South Vietnamese forces.

This dark, dangerous underground labyrinth was infested with rats and snakes, and full of disease such as malaria. The entrances and underpasses were often bombed and gassed by US forces. The bombing consisted of many tons of firepower on Cu Chi, but ultimately to little avail, as the network was long and vast and often easily rebuilt.

You can visit and tour the safer parts of the various tunnels today that have been widened and made taller for tourists—although they are not the same as they were during the war era. The visit requires at least half a day, so it might not be the best choice for travelers with only a few days in Ho Chi Minh City unless there is a special interest. There is a bus you can take to Cu Chi if you prefer to visit on your own. There are also tour groups available that include transportation. Private drivers can be booked through your hotel or through various travel agents.

There are two entrances to the tunnels, Ben Dinh and Ben Duoc. Most tourists visit Ben Dinh as this entrance is twenty minutes closer to Ho Chi Minh City, although it is the more crowded of the two. Entry to either is around $5 USD. There are tour guides on site if you come on your own outside of an organized tour.

Central Post Office
(2 Cong Xa Paris, District 1)
07:00 – 19:00 (until 18:00 weekends), daily, free

The Ho Chi Minh City Central Post Office, completed in 1891, is located in the city center of District 1 near the Notre Dame Cathedral Basilica. It is one of the grander examples of neo-Baroque architecture from the French colonial period in Vietnam. The building was designed by colonial architect Alfred Foulhoux, who is also responsible for several other 19th century edifices throughout the city.

The building was designed to showcase the advancement of science and technology at the time. This is evidenced by the large clock and the window plaque that lists the names of several of the leading scientists of the age.

Inside the post office there is a large portrait of Ho Chi Minh. There are also two large maps on the walls of appreciable interest, including one from 1936 showing telegraphic lines between various locations in Vietnam and Cambodia (*Cambodge* in French). The other is a regional map from 1892 showing Saigon and its surrounding area.

You can buy postcards and gifts, send mail, and sometimes even buy sim cards within the building. There are ATMs available inside the converted phone booths.

Opera House
(**www.hbso.org.vn**) (7 Lam Son Square, District 1)
No public tours, ticket office open daily

The Opera House was opened in 1900 with eight hundred seats and became the center of life for French colonialists. Like its larger sister building in Hanoi, the design was inspired by the venerable Palace Garnier in Paris (one of the more famous opera houses in the world, which also served as the original setting for the mighty

Phantom of the Opera). It is adjacent to the center of Dong Khoi Street, a tree-lined boulevard reminiscent of Paris. Its steps are a great place to relax and watch the traffic whir by.

Opera House at night (Efired/Shutterstock.com)

Originally, because of the intense heat in the city, the theater was only open for four months a year (October to January). At other periods of the year, it would have been too uncomfortably hot to sit through a performance.

In 1944, the Opera House was damaged during Allied bombing attacks against the occupying Japanese. In 1954, it was used as a shelter for French colonial citizens after the Viet Minh defeated the French at Dien Bien Phu.

From 1956-1975, the building was used as the lower house of the South Vietnamese Assembly. In 1975, after the Vietnam War, it became a theater once again.

It was restored and renovated in 1998 and today has a classier presentation. It is now used for conferences and various live theatrical performances. It is only open to the public during events and performances, not for touring. Its current name is the Ho Chi Minh

City Municipal Theater. Tickets may be found at the website (free ticket delivery) or **www.ticketbox.vn**.

City Hall
(86 Le Thanh Ton, District 1)
No public tours

This colonial-style structure, renamed the Ho Chi Minh City People's Committee Building in 1975, was completed in 1908. Its design and construction at the northern end of Nguyen Hue Boulevard was based on the Hotel de Ville (means "city hall" in French) in Paris, France. It is also known as the Hotel de Ville de Saigon. While the building is an active government center and is not open to the public (it is the seat of local government), admiring the architecture of one of Ho Chi Minh City's famous landmarks is an impressive and memorable experience. It is especially spectacular at night while the floodlights are on.

City Hall at night (Elena Ermakova/Shutterstock.com)

War Remnants Museum

(**warremnantsmuseum.com**) (28 Vo Van Tan, District 3)
07:30 – 12:00, 13:00 – 17:30, daily, adults: 15,000 VND

The War Remnants Museum is an exhibit focused primarily on the US-Vietnam War (there are some images from Vietnam's colonial period as well). State-operated, there is a selective use of horrific photos to paint a specific narrative of Vietnam's wartime history. The controversial museum primarily depicts the United States as the tyrannical, brutal oppressor of the Vietnamese among a world of vocal opposition. The pictures and moments they depict, however, are indeed appallingly real. If you visit, study the pictures, think about the time period and the various players, including a politically divided United States, the Chinese, the Soviet Union, and the North and South Vietnamese, all against the backdrop of the larger Cold War. Reflect upon motivations and draw your own conclusions.

Originally, the museum was called the Exhibition House for US and Puppet Crimes and at one time was also called the Museum of American War Crimes. Its latest name, the War Remnants Museum, was chosen as a less combative and controversial name as relations with the United States have become more fully restored.

In addition to the various disturbing images, you can also see up-close tanks, helicopters, fighter planes, daisy-cutter bombs, and other unexploded bombs from the Vietnam War era. There is also a building that reproduces the tiger cages used by the South Vietnamese as jail cells during the Vietnam War.

Ho Chi Minh City Museum

(**www.hcmc-museum.edu.vn**) (65 Ly Tu Trong, District 1)
08:00 – 17:00, daily, adults: 15,000 VND

The neo-classical building itself, completed in 1890, might be more fascinating than the actual contents of the museum. Between 1890 and 1945, it served as a residence to twenty-nine different governors and lieutenant governors of France's colonial Cochinchina where it was known as Gia Long Palace. For a short time in 1945, it became the Saigon home of Emperor Bao Dai of Vietnam, whose primary residence was in Hue. Later in 1945, following the return of French colonialism after Japan's surrender in the Second World War, it was reestablished as a residence for a French official. In 1955, South Vietnam President Ngo Dinh Diem established it as a reception hall for visiting foreign officials. After the attempted coup bombing of Norodom Palace, which was being demolished for the building of a new official structure, (where Reunification Palace now stands), Diem used this building as his residence. He had secret underground escape tunnels built in the event there would be another attempted overthrow. This secret construction became prophetic as he used these tunnels to escape this building during another coup attempt but was captured and assassinated the very next day in Cholon. After the fall of Saigon in 1975, the new government turned the building into a museum.

On the grounds outside the museum, you will find Soviet anti-aircraft guns, a Soviet tank, a fighter jet, and other vehicles and weapons of destruction used during the Vietnam War. Inside, there are several different rooms depicting life during the Vietnam War, the revolutionary struggle with France, and other artifacts from different periods during Ho Chi Minh City's history.

Fine Arts Museum
(97 Pho Duc Chinh, District 1)
09:00 – 17:00, Tuesday-Sunday, adults: 10,000 VND

Established in 1987, the Fine Arts Museum is a curated collection of Vietnamese art located within two large, splendidly grand French villas. The buildings themselves are masterpieces, combining elements of French colonial architecture with Chinese architectural components (the owner during colonial times was Chinese).

Several beautiful Vietnamese paintings can be enjoyed within the museum

With several floors and corridors of exhibits in each building (and a third building that is open from time to time), the Ho Chi Minh City Fine Arts Museum is a pleasure to visit. An easy five-minute walk from Ben Thanh Market, the museum can be visited in one to two hours, depending on your appetite for art appreciation.

The collection is mostly contemporary oil paintings, sculptures, and some relics from the Cham and Khmer eras. Many of the paintings are stunning in their use of color, capture of emotion, and vivid depiction of realism. A large percentage of these can be interpreted to be in support of not only the resistance to colonial forces, but also the North Vietnamese war effort to unify Vietnam under communism.

Cholon
(District 5)

Cholon, spelled as *Cho Lon* ("big market") in Vietnamese, is essentially the Chinatown of Ho Chi Minh City. It covers half of District 5 and a swath of District 6. It is a twenty-minute taxi ride (around 100,000 VND) from District 1 into Cholon. The area is known for Binh Tay Market, larger than the famous Ben Thanh Market in District 1, and catering more to locals than tourists. You won't find as many souvenirs here. It is more of a wholesale market, so prices tend to be cheaper. Many merchants in Ben Thanh Market come here for their wholesale purchases and transport their merchandise back to Ben Thanh Market, marking them up for sale to tourists.

This part of Ho Chi Minh City is older than the commercial center of District 1. Originally, Chinese inhabited this area alongside the Khmer people present here even before the Vietnamese settled from Hue to take control of today's southern Vietnam. It became a magnet for the Chinese when many were forced to leave the Bien Hoa area north of Ho Chi Minh City, as many were massacred when the Tay Son rulers of the time retaliated against those supporting the Nguyen lords. The Chinese came to Cholon and built high embankments along the Saigon River and settled. These embankments were called *Tai Ngon* in the Chinese dialect. There is a school of thought that the name for these embankments was the inspiration for the city's earlier name of Saigon.

The ethnic Chinese came into Vietnam across many time periods and for many different reasons. This population included many scholars, merchants, those seeking employment (especially during the French Colonial period in Vietnam), and refugees from various conflicts in China.

There was a major migration period out of China when the Ming dynasty fell in the 17th century and another significant influx during the Chinese Civil War in the middle of the 20th century. In the latter, Chinese nationalists were escaping Mao Zedong after defeat to the Chinese communists.

Many of the inhabitants of Cholon were of both Vietnamese and Chinese descent as the populations intermarried over time. The children tended to take on Chinese culture more than following Vietnamese tradition. They still regarded themselves as Chinese and often remained living within the district as adults.

As a merchant class, the Chinese of Cholon controlled 80 percent or more of the business in Saigon in the city's developing years. Despite this large presence, from time to time they have been forced by law to submit to various forms of assimilation, including in the 1950s when President Diem of the Republic of South Vietnam required the locals of Cholon to change their surname to a Vietnamese name within six months, or else risk heavy fines. After 1975, many ethnic Chinese left and returned to China or emigrated elsewhere after their businesses were confiscated by the new ruling party after the fall of Saigon. Today, in the Pasadena area of Southern California for example, there is an enclave of Cholon-originating Vietnamese immigrants of Chinese descent. Many emigrated to Chinatown in New York City as well.

While Cholon is likely not on the A-list of places to visit if you only have a few days in Ho Chi Minh City, the area can make for an intriguing half-day excursion if you have five days or more on your Ho Chi Minh City itinerary. You might also visit it as part of the various tours on offer in the city. You will see much Chinese decor and culture if you wander the backstreets. Cholon provides an opportunity to see a different aspect of the local culture from what you will experience in District 1 and other parts of Ho Chi Minh City.

There are several sights in Cholon in addition to the Binh Tay Market, including the Thien Hau Temple (Taoist) and the Quan Am Pagoda. There is also the Cha Tam Catholic Church here where President Diem was arrested before his assassination.

This area of Ho Chi Minh City was additionally famous as a black market for US Army personnel during the Vietnam War for various supplies. It is notorious as the location where four Australian journalists were killed during the Tet Offensive in 1968.

Bui Vien Street
(District 1, near Pham Ngu Lao)

For an electric and unique experience, visit "foreigner central" on Bui Vien Street. Grab a chair and a cheap beer and prepare for some fascinating people-watching and intense nightlife. Fire breathers, street peddlers of all sorts, edible dried squid vendors with bike carts, and having-a-good-time citizens (including many backpackers) from around the world troll back-and-forth on this street nightly. You will find bright neon signs, energetic bars (a few with live music), night clubs, local Vietnamese barbecue joints, street food vendors, beer swilling pubs, massage parlors, and boutique (some of which are seedy) hotels. Budget backpackers can find accommodations on this street and nearby Pham Ngu Lao. If a New Orleans Bourbon Street atmosphere "Saigon style" sounds like a blast, then you will surely enjoy an evening on Bui Vien.

Bitexco Financial Tower
(**www.saigonskydeck.com**) (2 Hai Trieu Street, District 1)
09:30 – 21:30, daily, adults: 200,000 VND

One of the more impressive architectural sights in Ho Chi Minh City is the Bitexco (a Vietnamese holding company operating in many different industries) Financial Tower. The tower is hard to miss as it is the tallest building in the city looming over the commercial center of District 1. Built in 2010, it was the tallest building in Vietnam at the time, towering sixty-eight stories. Two buildings in Hanoi, however, have been built since that are taller. Soon, it will no longer be the tallest building in Ho Chi Minh City, as a new building called Landmark 81 is scheduled to be completed in 2018 that will reach even higher into the sky.

The building, designed and completed by Venezuelan and French architects, drew its architectural inspiration from the lotus, Vietnam's national flower. Because of the curves, no two floors are exactly alike. There is a helipad (Vietnam's first) built on the fifty-second floor. Wind patterns and turbulence, however, have made it impossible for helicopters trying to land there. The elevator moves at seven meters per second—close to some of the fastest elevator speeds in the world.

There is an observation deck, and for approximately ten US dollars you can obtain some spectacular views of the city. If that price seems exorbitant, you can get similar views, along with some expensive coffee and desserts, from Café EON on the fiftieth floor inside the Bitexco Financial Tower without having to pay the observation deck fee.

There are a handful of casual restaurants inside and around the tower as well, including occasional live music. The first few floors have shopping, cafes, snacks, and a cinema. There is also a nightclub up high near the helipad (see *Nightlife*).

Fito Museum

(**www.fitomuseum.com.vn**) (41 Hoang Du Khuong, District 10)
08:30 – 17:00, Monday-Saturday, adults: 120,000 VND

The Fito Museum is dedicated to traditional Vietnamese medicine and herbs. It is a bit outside of town and is owned by the Fito Pharmaceutical Company. The museum also includes displays for Chinese traditional medicine.

Ho Chi Minh City Zoo

(**www.saigonzoo.net**) (2B Nguyen Binh Khiem, District 1)
07:00 – 18:30, daily, adults: 10,000 VND

Controversial to some because of its insufficient, older animal enclosures, the Ho Chi Minh City Zoo consists of well-manicured gardens and a diversity of animals such as tigers, elephants, crocodiles, monkeys, giraffes, rhinos, deer, wildebeests, a collection

of birds, varieties of snakes such as the Burmese python, and many animal breeds. The nearby river helps cool things off.

There is also the Museum of Vietnam History on the property, which provides an examination of various historical events from the Paleolithic era to the present, including a walkthrough exhibit showcasing the history of many of Vietnam's ruling dynasties.

Thich Quang Duc Memorial
(Corner of Cach Mang Thang Tam and Nguyen Dinh Chieu, District 3)
Outdoor exhibit, daily, free

Unveiled in 2010 and not far from Reunification Palace, this is a striking and peaceful memorial to Thich Quang Duc, the Buddhist monk. In 1963 Thich Quang Duc self-immolated at this intersection to protest what he considered the harsh mistreatment of Buddhists under the regime of President Diem during the Vietnam War. Covered in gasoline while sitting on the street, he struck a match and ignited himself as the gathered crowd watched in horror.

Skeptics claim these and other suicides were propagandized events, hence the presence of a tipped-off media ready with their cameras to disseminate photos and video of the event to global audiences. Scholars still debate the cause, motivation, and purpose of these suicides and whether they were a legitimate response to the alleged mistreatment, or carefully encouraged and orchestrated for political gain, as unfathomable as it may sound.

Regardless, this and other similar suicides that occurred throughout Vietnam were a terrible tragedy. It is difficult to comprehend the tremendous courage and sense of self-sacrifice such an act would require, whatever the motive of the individual monk. These self-immolations had a profound effect on world opinion and were an instrumental component in the rationale behind the subsequent military coup that resulted in the overthrow and assassination of President Diem. The gruesome video of the event, if you have the stomach for such a thing, can be found on YouTube and other video websites.

Getting Around

Getting around Ho Chi Minh City can be difficult at times, if not downright frightening. Here are a few suggestions and options for moving about the city.

Walking

Unless doing a guided tour or traveling a short distance, walking around town is best avoided. Often, the sidewalks are in disrepair and can be blocked by motorbikes and makeshift vendors. The air quality is poor in Ho Chi Minh City, and the less you breathe in, especially on a longer stay, the better. Also, the heat can drain your energy rather quickly. Sadly, you might also become a target for a thief or thieves on a motorbike who might try to swipe purses, bags, and mobile phones as they pass. Be aware that this can happen.

You will also discover that many motorbikers will ride on sidewalks and even speed around sidewalk corners. Be extremely cautious. Also, motorbikes will assume they have the right of way and several will disobey traffic signals. Do not count on them always stopping at red lights. As the Vietnamese say, only "tourists" walk in Ho Chi Minh City.

Crossing the Street

This is a notorious exercise not only in Ho Chi Minh City, but all of Vietnam. Sometimes you will have to cross the street. It can be quite hair-raising at times and will take some getting used to, as many intersections do not provide pedestrian crosswalks. When crossing on foot in these scenarios, if possible, wait until the road is clear. If there is an endless stream of motorbikes, find one of the larger gaps and begin walking. Pay close attention but keep walking smoothly and without sudden movement. The motorbikers will likely provide an opening for you as they go around you. Keep moving along at a consistent pace. DO NOT expect cars, buses, vans, or taxis to stop or give you the right of way. Watch others negotiate the traffic on foot a few times crossing the street before you attempt it yourself. If you are in any way immobile, and if it is necessary to cross the street, use extreme caution. Regardless of your physical status, be immensely careful, as pedestrian accidents and even death do occur and are unfortunately all too common throughout Ho Chi Minh City.

Taxis

If you hail a taxi, use either the Vinasun or Mai Linh taxi companies when possible. Often, you will find a uniformed person that works for either company that will hail a taxi for you and give you a slip of paper with the vehicle number in the event there are any shenanigans to report or if you leave something in the vehicle. Taxi drivers from these two companies are considerably less likely to run up the meter on tourists and are more reliable. There are lots of unauthorized taxis around town, and sometimes they will even try to deceive potential customers by using similar color schemes to masquerade as one of these two companies. Look closely to make sure the logos are correct before getting in when you hail one. Many of the other companies might also have honest taxi drivers, but in general they can be risky. Some locals suggest avoiding all but Vinasun and Mai Linh. If you suspect your meter is going up surprisingly and unexpectedly fast, stop the driver, get out, and find a new one. Most fares around District 1 should be in the 12,000 to 40,000 dong range unless you are traveling from one end of the district all the way to the other, in which case it might be a little more.

Uber

Uber is an attractive alternative to other forms of transportation in the city. It does require registering via your mobile phone with the service in advance; however, it will work with local sim cards that have a data plan and also with international data plans, as Internet access is all that is required to use the service. Uber is preferred by many because the meter is controlled by a central computer preventing any meter run-ups. You can watch the route on your mobile device to ensure you are traveling the quickest way to your destination. Furthermore, you have a record of the name and number of the driver if something is left in the vehicle or you have a complaint to report. Like in many major cities, the nascent Uber is experiencing some regulatory battles in Vietnam. It may or may not be an option during your trip.

Cyclos

Cyclos have been around Ho Chi Minh City since French colonial times. They look like a one- or two-seater chair with three wheels and a driver pedaling behind controlling its direction. They can be a convenient, open-air way to travel around town. Unfortunately, the operators do have a reputation of being unscrupulous from time to time. Be sure fares are clearly agreed upon before climbing aboard. Within District 1, fares should be within the 15,000 to 40,000 VND range. Insist that the driver stick to the agreed upon fee when disembarking.

Xe Om

Vietnamese for "motorbike hug," *xe om* are essentially motorbike taxis that many locals use. You will often see a man, sometimes young and sometimes old, resting on the seat of his motorbike waiting for a passenger. Occasionally, you will be approached by *xe om* drivers asking if you need a ride somewhere. If you oblige, be sure to negotiate all fares in advance in a manner similar as with the cyclo drivers. Also, only go with *xe om* drivers who provide you with a helmet for safety. These motorbikes travel with more speed than cyclos, therefore they are better suited for longer distances. The ride can be a little more startling at times with the heavy traffic, especially since you are with an unfamiliar driver. There is also no sanctioning or certification for these drivers. It can be a risky proposition and probably best avoided.

Vietnamese Language

In Vietnam today, there are over eighty-five million speakers of the Vietnamese language and its many dialects. In the US, it is the sixth most widely spoken language, largely because of the influx of refugees and immigrants from the Vietnam War during the 1970s. It is in the Austroasiatic family of languages (if you are a linguist) with significant Chinese, Khmer, later French and now English influence.

In parallel with the regional cuisine of Vietnam, there are three major regional dialects of the language spoken in Vietnam. These are the northern, central, and southern dialects. Within each of the three regions there are subregions and subdialects, some of them differing significantly from each other in expression and vocabulary. Regional and tribal languages also exist within Vietnam that are unintelligible when compared with the mother Vietnamese tongue.

There is good news regarding the Vietnamese language for English speakers. While the ancient Vietnamese language used modified Chinese characters similar to modern Chinese for its formal writing, today's Vietnamese language uses a Latin alphabet, making it one of the easier Asian languages for Westerners to understand and learn.

The reason for the Latin alphabet, known as *quoc ngu*, is that French missionaries (based on the work of prior Portuguese missionaries in Vietnam) developed a Romanized script for teaching religion to the local Vietnamese. This script captured the sounds and words most often used in the traditional Vietnamese language. Even though French was the official language of government administration during colonial times, *quoc ngu* began to serve as the standard written method of communication between French colonials and the city-dwelling Vietnamese with whom they came in to contact. By the early 20th century, its adoption was widespread and in use by nearly everyone in the country.

The standard Latin alphabet as the basis of the written form of the modern Vietnamese language is only part of the lexical puzzle. There are also important diacritical marks used heavily in the language. These marks not only help in the phonetic pronunciation of individual words, they are critical in distinguishing various words from each other. This is important as many unrelated words share the same spelling, but are pronounced differently, and therefore have entirely different meanings.

Here are the "letters" of the Vietnamese alphabet:

A Â Ă B C CH D Đ E Ê G GH GI H I K KH L M N NG NGH NH O Ô Ơ P PH QU R S T TH TR U Ư V Y

In some cases, there are multiple sounds present in the Vietnamese language represented by the same letters. For example, the "D" letter without a diacritic makes a "Z" sound, while the "Đ" makes a standard English-like hard "D" sound. The addition of diacritical marks in the Vietnamese alphabet indicates different standard pronunciations. While learning the language is beyond the scope of this book, seeing the alphabet helps to better understand the use of Romanized letters in Vietnamese. However, the use of diacritical marks is not limited to distinguishing letters of the alphabet.

Vietnamese, like Chinese, is a tonal language. This means the way that you inflect certain words during pronunciation is of critical importance. There are six different tones used in the Vietnamese language. Anyone studying or learning Vietnamese will need to become meticulously familiar with these tones, both in speaking and in writing (and it can be especially helpful with pronunciation). Using the wrong tone for a word will cause people not to understand what is being said, and you might experience blank looks for even the simplest of requests.

Diacritical marks are also used to indicate which tone is to be used. The six different tones in use in the Vietnamese language as follows:

- A *mid-level, flat* tone (for example: **ma** - means "ghost"); no mark
- A *low falling* tone (for example: **mà** - means "but"); note the downward diacritical mark
- A *high rising* tone (for example: **má** - means "mother")

- A *mid falling and then rising* tone (for example: **mả** - means "grave" or "tomb")
- A *high broken rising* tone (for example: **mã** - means "horse" - note: antiquated word)
- A *low falling broken* tone (for example: **mạ** - means "rice plant")

Not all combinations of spellings will have a separate word for all six tones, as *ma* is unusual in this way.

Fortunately, the Vietnamese language as written is an entirely phonetic representation of spoken words and usage. Mastering the alphabet and the use of these diacritical marks will help you gain a solid understanding of the language, at least to the extent possible by a non-native speaker.

Sometimes when texting using a smartphone or other device, Vietnamese people may omit these diacritical marks and draw meaning from the context of a sentence, as it can be time-consuming to enter the marks with mobile computing devices. Use of these marks however is otherwise essential in all formal Vietnamese writing.

Here are some basic words and expressions in Vietnamese that might be helpful to learn.

cam on (cam unh) - thank you
ăn - (an) to eat
uống - (oong) to drink
chào - (chow) hello
tôi là - (toy la) I am…/my name is...
vâng - (vung) yes
không - (khomb) no
Mỹ - (mee-ee) America
xin lỗi - (sin lo-ee) excuse me/I am sorry
nước - (new-uhk) water
sữa - (sue-uh) milk
bia - (bee-uh) beer
tôi muốn - (toy moon) I want...
một ít - (mote eet) a little
một - (mote) one
hai - (hi) two
ba - (baa) three

For further study, *Pimsleur Vietnamese* (available at **www.pimsleur.com**) is a language course with downloadable material that can help you get started learning to be conversant. It is especially useful for learning pronunciation. The *Rosetta Stone* language series' immersion and visual approach is also a useful tool for gaining a foothold on vocabulary and usage. Like most Vietnamese learning tools on the market, however, the focus of both of these products is on the northern (Hanoi) dialect of the Vietnamese language rather than the southern dialect (although many Vietnamese understand both dialects). Even so, working your way through several of the lessons will be helpful in your language appreciation and provide some fun, as the Vietnamese people take great delight in foreigners attempting to speak their language.

Cuisine of the City

"When eating the fruit, think of who planted the tree." –
Vietnamese Proverb

Regional Cuisine of Vietnam

Ho Chi Minh City, and to a larger extent the entire country of Vietnam, enjoys one of the more exciting, inventive, and energetic culinary scenes found anywhere in the world. From the enchanting street food and its open-flame, charcoal grill-based delicacies to elegant villa, colonial-era multi-course delightfulness, the diversity of dining is extraordinary. You will discover various fresh seafood, flavorful beef dishes, and creative, complex soup dishes. Each of these contains a unique palette of flavors that includes mysterious vegetables, herbs, spices, and exotic fruits. Meals are prepared with many different cooking styles and based on ancient oriental techniques. The infinite combination of flavors, fresh vegetables, fish, meats, sauces, and oil-free flame cooking will leave you longing for more once you arrive back home. The cuisine scene in Ho Chi Minh City might be the city's best and most rewarding attraction.

To first understand the complexity and landscape of Ho Chi Minh City's palate, it is important to understand the entire Vietnamese culinary landscape. There is an abundance of food source diversity in Vietnam including mountains, forests, jungle, thousands of miles of oceanic coastline, and two major river deltas, all distributed throughout various different climates. These abundant resources, combined with the range of ethnic groups (there are fifty-four) in Vietnam, and their contributions to the country's kitchen, create an exciting foundation to one of the world's greatest and unique gastronomies. There is also significant influence from China, and to a lesser extent, Indian, French, and other Western influences that help enrich local dishes and provide the basis for Vietnam's emerging prestige on the global culinary stage.

There are three major regions of cuisine in Vietnam. Each of these regions shares *nuoc mam*, translated to fish sauce, as the foundation of their respective local menus. *Nuoc mam* is created from the fermentation of fish (usually anchovies) with sea salt. Its creation requires a production process that takes years and results in a brownish-amber liquid. While most prevalent in Vietnam, its use in Southeast Asia extends beyond its borders to nearby Thailand, Laos, and Cambodia. *Nuoc mam* is rarely used pure, but instead is combined with herbs, salt, pepper, sugar, and chilies. It is then diluted with water to create a dipping sauce known as *nuoc cham* for use with a broad range of dishes. In addition to this *nuoc mam* staple, rice is the other major component of the Vietnamese table.

The three major regional cuisines of Vietnam are the northern cuisine (primarily around Hanoi and the Red River Delta), the central and highlands cuisine (around and commonly referred to as from the cities of Hue and Hoi An), and the southern cuisine (including Ho Chi Minh City and the Mekong Delta). Each of these is as distinct as the region's people, available ingredients, and weather patterns. You typically won't find butter, cream, or alcohol in any of these three regional traditions, but instead will encounter fresh, organic ingredients, piquant marinades, and short cooking times. Almost all dishes include uncooked herbs and spices that electrify flavor.

The first of the three regional categories, the northern Hanoi-based cuisine, is rich in tradition. Its character is driven by its climate. Unlike the other two regions of the country, the north enjoys four distinct seasons. It is considered rustic or country Vietnamese by some because of the extensive use of seasonal vegetables, herbs, and freshwater fish from its rivers. The renowned sour and complexly flavored beef noodle soup and national dish *pho* is believed to have originated in Hanoi, perhaps with some French and Cantonese influences. The region is also known for other famous dishes such as *cha ca*, a grilled catfish dish flavored with dill; *banh cuon*, a soft, stuffed, and fermented, soft rice flour-cooked roll; and *nem ran*, a flavorful fried spring roll containing pork sausage. There is a focus on texture and complementary flavors in northern cuisine. There is recognizably less spiciness to the dishes than those you will find in other parts of Vietnam.

Next is the cuisine of central Vietnam. These dishes are often spicy and contain lots of fresh and salt water fish, including shellfish. Once the capital of ancient Vietnam and still known as the Imperial City, the cuisine of Hue (pronounced "hway"–rhymes with "day") has a royal heritage. This haute cuisine primarily consists of several small dishes with an elegantly refined and creative presentation. Emperor Tu Duc, who reigned in the late 1800s, insisted that meals consist of fifty individual dishes to be cooked by fifty chefs and served by fifty servants. This heritage is reflected today in the creative, tasting-menu-oriented dishes served in Hue (and at many "Hue food" restaurants in Ho Chi Minh City).

Also, *bun bo Hue*, or Hue-style beef vermicelli soup, is an incredibly flavorful classic soup from the region that you will find throughout Ho Chi Minh City. Many modest restaurant shops specialize in this offering. Trying and comparing it with its classic counterpart *pho* is a must for any connoisseur of Vietnamese cuisine.

Banh xeo, another Vietnamese classic, is essentially a stuffed crispy pancake that originates from this region. *Xeo* (pronounced "say-oh") means "sizzle" and the pancakes are often cooked in beer to obtain the proper, crisp texture.

Due to Buddhist beliefs, many of the dishes of Hue are vegetarian dishes, which in turn necessitate a lot of flavor. Hue food can be quite spicy as well.

The central Vietnamese menu, however, is not defined only by the dishes of Hue; the coastal towns of Nha Trang and Hoi An contribute significantly with their own innovations. Nha Trang lobster and other coastal dishes, such as the *cao lau* (pork, noodle, and fresh greens) of Hoi An, also serve as part of the gastronomical fabric of the region and are well-known throughout Vietnam.

Finally, the cuisine of the south is heavily dominated by the influence of the Mekong Delta and its intense tropical climate. Coconuts, pineapples, limes, and other flavorsome fruits grow abundantly in the region, as do chilies, lemongrass, sugarcane, and other staples of the culinary south. Also, plentiful rice paddies throughout southern Vietnam contribute significantly to the Ho Chi

Minh City menu of offerings, providing rice in many forms including rice noodles and rice paper.

The many soup entrees of Ho Chi Minh City are known for their sweet and sour broths. The cuisine in general is highlighted by its balance of sweetness, sourness, and spiciness. *Goi cuon*, or "summer rolls," are softened rice paper rolls stuffed with pork, shrimp, cilantro, mint, and fermented carrot, that are then dipped in a *nuoc cham* fish sauce, or alternatively a spicy peanut sauce. They are a regional classic. Also, sweet and sour fish soups and smoking hot, street-cooked snails are famous in the region. Because of Khmer roots and proximity to the traditions of the Mekong River, curry finds its way into some local dishes as well.

French influence is prevalent in Ho Chi Minh City, not only in its coffee shop culture, but in the origins of the *banh mi* sandwich, a world-famous baguette hoagie served with local Vietnamese ingredients such as pork, spicy pâté, cilantro, fermented carrots, and daikon. The flavorful sandwich is gaining in popularity worldwide.

Experiencing these three major regional approaches to the dinner table will underscore the great depth and complexity that is the Vietnamese palate. In Ho Chi Minh City, you will have the opportunity to experience many of the traditional dishes that have permeated all of Vietnam for centuries. You will also discover contemporary versions of these same flavors, sometimes in social street food settings, and other times tucked away in beautiful, elegantly appointed villa-turned-restaurants with teakwood tables, bamboo chairs, and ceiling fans, all combining for a timeless sensation of dining in the aristocratic, colonial past. Explore as much Vietnamese cuisine as you can. Chances are, it will leave its indelible imprint on you like it has on so many who have gone before.

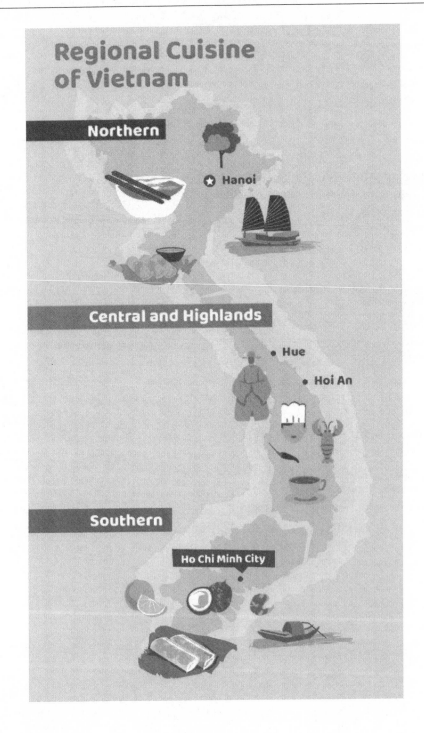

Classic Dishes to Try

Here is a sample collection of favorite dishes found in homes, restaurants, and among street vendors throughout Ho Chi Minh City. While this list is far from exhaustive, it does contain several well-known, traditional dishes and provides for a substantive foundational knowledge of the classic fare served in and around the city. It is an important primer for your culinary experiences to come. Be sure to try several of these dishes, and in as many variations as you can find.

Pho (pronounced "foe-oh": unbroken, falling then rising tone)

Pho, the world-famous flavorful, ingredient-rich, simmering-broth beef noodle soup, is the national dish of Vietnam. While there is some historical dispute, a common theory is that the dish is an evolution of the French dish *pot-au-feu* (pot on the fire) introduced to northern Vietnam during the French colonial period. The original French *pot-au-feu* consisted of various cuts of beef, carrots, turnips, onions, potatoes, and spices that cooked for long hours in a pot over a fire. The proponents of this version of the dish's evolution contend that the Vietnamese took this dish, used leftover bones to flavor the soup because of the lack of available beef (cows were not traditionally slaughtered in those days by the Vietnamese for meat but rather used for farming assistance), and combined the broth with noodles, other local ingredients, and local herbs and spices for a uniquely Vietnamese version. The dish then evolved over a century to the famous *pho* enjoyed globally today. Some claim, however, that the dish is Cantonese in origin. Others insist that it is a uniquely Vietnamese improvisation. Perhaps its evolution can be explained with contribution from all three theories.

While its origin is in northern Vietnam, *pho* is a remarkably popular street food dish in Ho Chi Minh City. It can be found everywhere, including in *pho*-dedicated restaurants, makeshift sidewalk cafes, and even with mobile street vendors. The southern version (*pho viet*) is somewhat different from the conventional northern version (*pho bac*), the former with a sweeter and sometimes sour broth, and utilizing garnishes such as lime, hoisin sauce, hot chili/sriracha sauce, cinnamon, cilantro, Thai basil, chilies, and bean sprouts. These garnishes, many of which come from the Mekong Delta region, are delivered on a plate alongside a bowl of *pho* and added as desired by the eater.

The soup itself takes several hours to make. Like in historical versions of the dish, the broth is made with beef bones and oxtail along with roasted onions and many different Vietnamese spices. As it slowly simmers, the bubbly top is often scraped away to ensure a clearer broth. A clear broth is accepted as a sign of a wonderfully flavored and fragrant soup. Rice noodles are added and cooked before serving.

There are several variations of *pho*, not only in the garnishes provided, but also within the dish itself. While the standard is *pho bo* (beef *pho*), other common variations include *pho ga* (chicken *pho*), *pho chin* (well-done beef *pho*) and *pho tai* (rare beef *pho*). *Pho tai* is likely the most famous and popular version of *pho* and perhaps the one you ought to try first as a baseline for comparison.

Southern Vietnam version of pho

Banh Mi (pronounced "bahn mee")

French colonial influence engendered the *banh mi* sandwich in Ho Chi Minh City, where the bold flavors of this region are packed into a Vietnamese baguette (made with both rice and wheat flour, making it somewhat different from its French bread counterpart). This stuffed baguette includes pork, Vietnamese sausage, spicy pâté, jalapenos, mayonnaise, cucumber, pickled carrot, daikon, and cilantro. It can also be made with other ingredients such as meatballs, chicken, or lemongrass beef. Not only is it a local street food favorite in Ho Chi Minh City, but the sandwich continues to gain a global reputation and is likely available somewhere in your hometown or nearby.

Banh Xeo (pronounced "bahn say-oh")

These fried, stuffed Vietnamese pancakes are named for the "sizzle" they make when cooking on the stove. There is a local, unofficial secret of using beer during the sizzling process to obtain the crispiness of the rice flour, water, and coconut milk-batter. When served, the pancakes are folded in half and filled with bean sprouts, fresh mint, Thai basil, and other herbs, and then wrapped within a mustard leaf before the diner is encouraged to dip the creation into a sweet and sour *nuoc cham* fish sauce.

Bun Bo Hue (pronounced "boon boe hweh")

Originating in Hue, but notably popular in Ho Chi Minh City, this spicy beef and rice noodle dish has balanced salty, spicy, and sour flavors of lemongrass, chilies, and lime. Its tangy red broth, beef brisket, soft noodles, occasionally a coagulated blood cube, and fresh herb garnishes make this a spectacular Vietnamese soup meal. It will surely someday give *pho* a run for the Vietnamese soup heavyweight title as it gains in popularity (but don't count out *bun rieu* either).

Bun bo Hue

Chao Tom (pronounced "chow tome" - rhymes with "home")

Shrimp paste served on sugarcane is another dish originating in central Vietnam that is a favorite in Ho Chi Minh City. In the southern version, shrimp is pounded into a paste with garlic and spices such as paprika and white pepper. The paste is then shaped and cooked on a sugarcane skewer. It is served with rice paper, vermicelli rice noodles (sometimes in the form of a square of plaid-patterned noodles), and various garnishes such as cilantro and fresh mint. Lastly, the paste is removed from the skewer, loaded with the garnishes and noodles, wrapped in rice paper, and then dipped into the requisite *nuoc cham* tangy fish sauce. This dish and its presentation is definitely a creative, regional classic in Hue imperial tradition.

Tom (pronounced "tome")

Charcoal-grilled shrimp-on-a-stick served exquisitely charred is a classic in Ho Chi Minh City. The fresh shrimp is normally skewered live, within its shell, and often marinated (and might even still be kicking if served raw in a barbecue-it-yourself restaurant). The fire-kissed shrimp tastes fresh and is wonderfully flavored. Dipping the shrimp into tiny bowls of salt, pepper, lime juice, and red chilies gives it a beautifully complex boost of flavor. After sampling this with the prescribed accompaniment, you might never use melted butter again with your shellfish. These go down well while swilling cold, local beer.

Shrimp (tom) skewered and cooked on a charcoal grill

Goi Cuon (pronounced "goy coon")

These famous rice paper rolls, sometimes known as "summer rolls" and other times as "salad rolls," are filled with shrimp, pork, pickled carrot shreds, cucumber slivers, mint, and other garnishes. They are then dipped into a spicy, tangy *nuoc cham* fish sauce for additional flavor. The freshness of Vietnam cuisine really shines through in this classic appetizer, and ought to be part of several meals while you are in Ho Chi Minh City (and when you arrive home as well). Don't be surprised if you often desire two or three orders of this classic, as it is an amazingly fresh and delicious appetizer. A spicy peanut sauce is sometimes substituted for the *nuoc cham*.

Fresh summer rolls (goi cuon)

Cha Gio (pronounced "cha zaw")

Also known as imperial rolls, these are essentially a Vietnamese version of deep fried spring rolls filled with regional, highly flavored ingredients, wrapped in a mustard leaf, and dipped into the traditional sweet, sour, and spicy fish sauce. It makes for a great appetizer. You can never have just one of these, as the combination of the piquant leaf, the hot spring roll, and the tangy *nuoc cham* provide an inescapable combination of flavors you will find yourself seeking out often while in Ho Chi Minh City.

Bun Thit Nuong (pronounced "boon tit noong")

This classic consists of charcoal-grilled lemongrass pork served over rice noodles with pickled carrots, cilantro, and a *cha gio* imperial spring roll. It is then drizzled in sweet, sour, and spicy *nuoc cham* fish sauce for tanginess. This popular medley of fresh ingredients might quickly become your favorite dish. The blend of flavors and texture help redefine what Asian noodle dishes can be. Often, crushed peanuts will be sprinkled over the top for additional texture and happiness.

Bo La Lot (pronounced "boe luh lote")

This wonderfully fragrant and flavorful beef dish is another one not to be missed. Minced beef and pork mixed with fresh lemongrass, five spice, garlic, shallots, and other various herbs are rolled and wrapped in fresh green betel leaves. These little masterpieces are then skewered and grilled over hot charcoal. This creates a unique and memorable taste as the leaves give off an herbal, peppery smell when cooked and are imparted as flavor to the meat. The beef rolls are then served with rice paper, vermicelli rice noodles, and various garnishes such as pickled carrot slivers, cilantro, and Thai basil to be wrapped in rice paper by the customer (essentially a roll within a roll). The resultant goodness is then hand-dipped into the sweet and spicy *nuoc cham* fish sauce. The combination of flavors in this dish is exciting, innovative, and unique. The dark green color of the charred betel leaves adds to the enjoyment of this visually compelling, tantalizing dish.

Bo la lot with wrapping accoutrements

Oc (pronounced "op")

Snail Street, also known as *Oc Street* in District 4, has become noteworthy in Ho Chi Minh City because of the many customer-frenzied snail joints that line the avenue. There are also several other locations throughout the city to find various types of snails roasting on charcoal grills and over open flame. You will see many types of freshwater snails in all different shapes and sizes on display at these various open-air restaurants, all of which are ready to be roasted over a blazing charcoal grill. Some of the snails are large and a small fork is ideal for pulling them out of the shell when cooked. Other snails are quite tiny and require a safety pin to dig the flavorful meat from the smoking tiny shell. These snails pair wonderfully with the cold, local beer you will find being guzzled in these eateries, as the revelry continues for hours each night. Arrive early though, as the snail selection dwindles significantly at most places by mid-evening.

Snails (oc) fresh off the grill

Nem Cua Be (pronounced "nem koo-uh bay")

Originally from the coastal town of Haiphong near Halong Bay in northeastern Vietnam, these exceptionally large spring rolls come fried and stuffed with crab meat. They also include pork, egg, vermicelli noodles, and several other vegetables. Sometimes they arrive from the kitchen not only piping hot, but so large that they need to be cut with scissors to make them bite size. Of course, the snipped pieces are to be dipped in the classic *nuoc cham* sauce prior to eating.

Crab stuffed jumbo spring rolls (nem cua be)

Bun Rieu (pronounced "boon rio")

This is another classic vermicelli rice noodle soup. Bowls are loaded with crab meat, shrimp paste, and many vegetables, all of which have been simmering together in a tomato broth. There are many variations of this soup. Along with *pho* and *bun bo Hue*, this soup represents the "big three" of Vietnamese hot and sour soups, although fans of *hu tieu* soup, also a popular soup of the Mekong Delta, might argue that there should be a "big four."

Bun rieu

Thit Nuong (pronounced "tit noong")

Lemongrass is an intensely fragrant tropical herb used often in Southeast Asian cooking, especially in Vietnam, for its flavor and aromatics. It is typically finely chopped. Along with the traditional grilled pork recipes for which this dish is named, lemongrass chicken is also a favorite. Many variations of lemongrass-based dishes exist. While pork and poultry flavored with lemongrass can be divine on their own, these preparations can also be used as components of a large number of other Vietnamese dishes, such as *bun thit nuong* described above.

Goi Du Du (pronounced "goy doo doo")

Few dishes capture the freshness of ingredients available in the Mekong Delta region such as green papaya salad. The shredded, unripe papaya is combined with lime juice, peanuts, fish sauce, dried shrimp, and palm sugar to create a bright, sour, refreshing culinary creation that is often enjoyed in other parts of Southeast Asia as well.

Xoi Ga (pronounced "soy gah")

This sticky, glutinous rice (*xoi*) served with chicken (*ga*) is a street favorite in Ho Chi Minh City and can make for a great lunch choice. Many restaurants specialize in this dish alone, with the term "*xoi ga*" in the name of the establishment. Chicken can be exceptionally tasty in Vietnam, as some of the local, organic chicken breeds provide juicy, flavorful meats. Steaming the chicken allows this unique flavor to be enjoyed in its simple, natural form. This makes for a perfect pairing with the sticky rice.

Banh Chuoi (pronounced "bon chewy")

Vietnamese banana cake makes for a great introduction to the desserts of Ho Chi Minh City. It is usually made with coconut milk, appears purplish in color, and is placed inside sticky rice and steamed inside a banana leaf (*banh tet chuoi*). You can find this dessert served in many restaurants, but some of the best are available from street vendors selling it in the banana-leaf-wrapped form. *Banh chuoi nuoc dua* is also a favorite, where the banana cake is slathered in warm, thick coconut milk and sprinkled with chopped peanuts.

Banana cake (banh chuoi) in coconut milk

Fruit of the Mekong Delta and Beyond

A wonderful gift Ho Chi Minh City receives because of its climate and proximity to the Mekong Delta is the great diversity and abundance of fruit available throughout the year. Fruit is a major component of many of Vietnam's dishes, especially southern Vietnam's traditional, organic cooking, and is sold fresh in markets everywhere.

Most of these fruits are seasonal with certain peak periods. Here is a list of local favorites to sample if available during your visit. While many of these delights come from the Mekong Delta, some are transported in from other parts of Vietnam, especially the cooler highlands.

Ambarella (*coc*) – Somewhat like a poor man's mango, this tropical fruit is especially enjoyable in smoothie-form with a flavor similar to a rich, spicy apple sauce. Ambarellas can be invitingly sweet when fully ripe.

Avocado (*trai bo*) – Introduced by the French and technically a fruit, Vietnamese avocados are especially wonderful in various dessert drinks on a hot afternoon in Ho Chi Minh City, including the avocado smoothie. This refreshing, flavorful concoction is made by blending ripe avocado with sweetened, condensed milk. Make trying one of these a priority on your visit.

Banana (*chuoi*) – Over a million tons of bananas per year are commercially produced in Vietnam. The many varieties available are components of various desserts, including *banh chuoi*, the classic Vietnamese banana cake. There are delectable sweet banana soups listed on many dessert menus. You can find local bananas being grilled over hot charcoal and smothered in warm coconut sauce at many street vendor stalls. You will find green, unripe bananas used, especially when rolled in rice paper, to provide texture and a sour, tannic flavor to many dishes. The flower of the banana tree is used in the banana flower salad. These flowers are also used to hold the contents of other dishes, like a small green bowl, as part of a serving presentation. Many sticky rice combinations and seafood items are grilled inside large banana leaves, in the latter case to impart special flavors to the fish.

Breast Fruit (*vu sua*) – Rare and prized, and looking like a half-ripe apple, the white flesh of this fruit emits a milky juice when bitten or cut. They are cut in half (don't bite the skin) and the flesh is carved out with a spoon. This fruit has a short season. Consider yourself lucky if you are able to sample these.

Coconut (*dua*) – Many street vendors around the city sell fresh coconut juice drinkable directly from the whole coconut (via a straw) after hacking off the top of the fruit. Coconut is used in many edible creations, including the wonderful warm coconut sauce used in many desserts. Coconut candy is a famous treat and is usually made by hand in the Mekong Delta. The leaves of coconut trees are used to thatch roofs in the countryside.

Dragon Fruit (*than long*) – This large cactus plant fruit looks like it is on fire from afar, or perhaps like a large pink artichoke. Originally from Central America and brought into Vietnam by the French, it was traditionally only eaten by the Vietnamese emperor. Its highly prized black speckled red or white sweet flesh is mostly eaten as a standalone, refreshing dessert.

Durian (*sau rieng*) – The potent smell of this infamous fruit with its custard-like flesh, similar to a ripe, pungent, soft cheese, has caused it to be banned from many hotel rooms and car rental companies. The taste can stay in your mouth for forty-eight hours or so. It is six times larger than a mango and can be quite expensive. Over a hundred of these can grow on a single tree.

Guava (*qua oi*) – With a pink or sometimes white flesh tasting similar to melon, guava will often be found as a fresh fruit juice beverage in Vietnam. You can also find guava candy in many markets.

Jackfruit (*mit*) – This is the largest tree-borne fruit in the world. Loaded with vitamins and minerals, its inner bulbs taste like pulled pork. In addition to being eaten raw, it is often used in cooking and in salads. As the fruit is quite large, it is usually cut into segments when sold at the market.

Lime (*chanh*) – Limes are a way of life in Vietnam. They are mostly combined with salt, chilies, and black pepper as a dipping sauce and to add an optional sourness to many dishes, including *pho*. When delivered to your table in a restaurant, they will often be cut slightly off-center. This asymmetry makes it easier to add the squeezed juice to your dish.

Longan (*nhan*) – A longan is a fruit cultivated primarily in the south of Vietnam and is similar to the lychee or rambutan. It is known by many as the "eye of the dragon" and is eaten for vitality. The fruit is round like a grape and similar in size. Its skin is inedible, but when peeled gives way to a sweet, juicy, translucent flesh.

Mango (*xoai*) – The best mangoes for eating are usually the ones with yellow skin. When fresh and juicy (and not too sour), these fruit are an amazingly refreshing and restorative treat to enjoy while in

Vietnam. They are often used in dessert dishes, such as mango sticky rice, even though that is more typically a Thai offering. The sour green unripe mango can be used in salads. There is a sweet green ripe mango variety that comes from Thailand that is present at many local markets.

Mangosteen (*mang cut*) – Cutting through the violet skin to the sweet, fragrant white flesh is quite a treat (but don't bite into the skin). It has just the right amount of sourness, balanced with a juicy lusciousness, that makes this one of the top fruit selections on offer in Vietnam. It is sometimes used in the making of ice cream or sorbet.

Papaya (*du du*) – An inexpensive fruit in Vietnam often used for dessert, papaya is sometimes an unripe component in salads and in soups. When ripe, it can be eaten raw or used for smoothies or other dessert drinks.

Passion Fruit (*chanh leo*) – Harvested year-round, this fruit is quite striking when its purple skin is cut through, revealing the yellowish-orange seeds inside. Often used for juicing, passion fruit makes for a great dessert when eaten with a spoon right out of its skin.

Persimmon (*hong*) – Looking like an orange tomato, this sweet fruit is usually sliced and eaten out of hand. It can be used for juicing and is often dried.

Pineapple (*dua*) – The familiar tropical pineapple is often eaten with chili salt in Vietnam, providing a "sweet heat" as a mid-afternoon snack or dessert. After bananas, the pineapple is the second most commercially produced fruit in Vietnam.

Pomelo (*buoi*) – Similar to a grapefruit, it is usually eaten raw (accompanied with chili salt) or sometimes used in a traditional pomelo salad. This is the largest of all citrus fruits.

Rambutan (*chom chom*) – This moderately-sized round fruit with red, prickly skin is similar to a lychee. Don't eat the encasing, as only the sweet, juicy flesh inside is the edible portion.

Sapodilla (*hong xiem*) – This egg-shaped fruit with brownish skin tastes like a combination of apples, bananas, and sometimes molasses when eaten raw. They are great for blending into smoothies.

Soursop (*mang cau*) – This fruit's thick green skin can be difficult to peel, and its yellowish-white flesh can be somewhat sour. It is mostly eaten raw but is also used for juicing or processed into a creamy texture for desserts.

Starfruit (*khe*) – Resembling a star, especially when sliced, this citrus-like fruit can be eaten raw, juiced for drinks, or used to provide texture and flavor to various dishes.

Strawberry (*dau tay*) – Strawberries in Vietnam only grow in the cooler highlands around Dalat, where they are used to make jam. They do make their way down to Ho Chi Minh City's markets when in season.

Watermelon (*dua hau*) – Considered a magic fruit by some in Vietnam, watermelons are beautifully carved and decorated for the annual Tet holiday. They are eaten raw from the rind, and sometimes can be sprinkled with chili salt for additional flavor.

Seasonal Fruit Chart

Fruit	Jan	Feb	Mar	Apr	May	Jun	Jul	Aug	Sep	Oct	Nov	Dec
Ambarella						Jun	Jul	Aug	Sep			
Avocado			Mar	Apr	May	Jun	Jul	Aug				
Banana	Jan	Feb	Mar	Apr	May	Jun	Jul	Aug	Sep	Oct	Nov	Dec
Breast Fruit	Jan	Feb									Nov	Dec
Coconut	Jan	Feb	Mar	Apr						Oct	Nov	Dec
Dragon Fruit	Jan	Feb	Mar			Jun	Jul	Aug	Sep	Oct	Nov	Dec
Durian					May	Jun	Jul	Aug				
Guava	Jan					Jun						
Jackfruit			Mar	Apr	May	Jun						
Lime	Jan	Feb	Mar	Apr	May	Jun	Jul	Aug	Sep	Oct	Nov	Dec
Longan					May	Jun	Jul	Aug	Sep	Oct		
Mango	Jan	Feb	Mar	Apr	May	Jun	Jul					
Mangosteen	Jan	Feb			May	Jun	Jul	Aug				
Papaya	Jan	Feb						Aug	Sep	Oct	Nov	Dec
Passion Fruit	Jan	Feb						Aug	Sep	Oct	Nov	Dec
Persimmon								Aug	Sep	Oct	Nov	
Pineapple				Apr	May	Jun	Jul	Aug			Nov	Dec
Pomelo	Jan	Feb				Jun	Jul	Aug	Sep	Oct	Nov	Dec
Rambutan					May	Jun	Jul	Aug				
Sapodilla	Jan	Feb	Mar									Dec
Soursop	Jan	Feb			May	Jun						
Starfruit				Apr	May	Jun				Oct	Nov	Dec
Strawberry		Feb	Mar	Apr								
Watermelon	Jan					Jun	Jul					Dec

Vegetable Culture

Vegetables, especially of the green variety, are quite bountiful in southern Vietnam. Like with fruit, the Mekong Delta region is fertile ground for an assortment of leafy delights. These vegetables are an important component of the region's fresh-tasting gastronomic treasures. Travel to any of the various food markets in Vietnam and you will see table after table with heaps of fresh vegetables on display, the hallmark of many Vietnamese dishes and the foundation of the masterful work of many local chefs. The innumerable kitchens of Ho Chi Minh City make great and varied use of the region's fertile river delta.

Unlike in China, many of the vegetables in Vietnam appear on the table fresh and as uncooked components, rather than wok-fried. This is in large part because much of Vietnamese cooking involves the charcoal grill instead of sizzling oil. This contributes to the reputation of a color-rich, healthy, lightness and brightness of flavor in many Vietnamese mealtime favorites. You will find this fresh vegetable-heavy approach more in Ho Chi Minh City than Hanoi, even though the Red River Delta region is another bountiful source of Vietnamese vegetables, many of which do end up in Ho Chi Minh City.

Pho for example, the national dish of Vietnam, along with freshly cut limes, is accompanied by several different greens and other vegetables when served in Ho Chi Minh City (different garnishes than in Hanoi). Your first local bowl of *pho* will clearly demonstrate the importance of fresh local vegetables to Vietnamese cooking. Chives, Thai basil (more pungent than Italian basil), bean sprouts, chilies, cilantro, and another Vietnamese herb known as culantro (*ngo gai* locally, and stronger and more pungent than its cousin cilantro) add a cornucopia of flavor to the broth when these garnishes are added to a dish by the dining customer.

You will find fresh mint, cucumber, cabbage, and lettuce as key components in *goi cuon*, the famous Vietnamese summer rolls. Called "salad rolls" by some (literal translation), it's the vegetable component that provides much of the flavor that has made this appetizer world famous.

Stir-frying still is a primary cooking method for standalone vegetable dishes. Chinese broccoli, bok choy, green beans, and water spinach (*rau muong*) are all examples of vegetables that can be cooked and served as side dishes. Taro stem (*doc mung*) is a component of many broths as well. It stars in *canh chua ca loc*, a famous regional sour vegetable soup. You are unlikely to find any of the region's famous soup dishes prepared and served without greens.

The Beverage Landscape

When it comes to beverages, Ho Chi Minh City also carries a great deal of diversity and uniqueness. First, because its many soup dishes are primarily in liquid form, there is often not a separate beverage to go along with a meal, as the soup provides the necessary hydration. Instead, a drink is ordinarily imbibed on its own, separate from a meal, and therefore is an elevated experience. Enjoying the multitude of beverages available in Ho Chi Minh City is frequently a cause for joining with friends.

Coffee of course is paramount. See *Coffee Shop Culture* for a more in-depth, comprehensive description of the coffee scene in Ho Chi Minh City and where to drink it.

Hot tea is another mainstay in Vietnam, including in Ho Chi Minh City. Green tea is by far the favorite. Lemongrass tea is another revered local choice. *Nuoc sam*, a local herbal tea, is worth seeking out as well.

Sweet drinks are another highlight in Ho Chi Minh City. Bubble tea, milk tea with tapioca, and the various coconut jelly drinks that can be found in places like Ben Thanh Market obscure the line between beverage and dessert. Multicolored "rainbow" drinks, often with coconut milk and ice, are a big hit in the heat of Ho Chi Minh City and available in many casual restaurants.

Fresh fruit juices are readily available throughout the city because of the local abundance of fruit in the Mekong Delta region. Fresh coconuts, often sold street-side and enjoyed directly from the actual coconut with a straw, are a must-try (and don't forget to dig out and eat the coconut flesh with a spoon when you finish the juice). Other refreshing options on scorching hot days include watermelon juice, mango juice, and passion fruit juice. Sugarcane juice, or *nuoc mia*, is spectacular as well, regularly chosen by locals because they believe it has a cooling effect once inside one's body and is rumored to be a hangover cure.

Smoothies are a flavorful, refreshing treat, especially in the intense heat. Avocado, mango, custard apple, sapodilla, and soursop are all top choices. Bird nest milk, generally found in a can, is another unique local beverage to try. Fresh, cold lemon soda is popular and usually available in most dining establishments.

As far as libations go, Ho Chi Minh City is mostly a beer town. Lager-style beers dominate the scene. While you will find tables full of men (and some women) pounding cold ones and stacking empty cans well into the night without any food, cold beer is a great match for many local dishes, and a great way to beat the evening heat. A great accompaniment for a cold brewski is a large, charcoal-grilled set of skewered prawns, peeled at the table and then dipped in a salt, black pepper, red chili, and lime juice mixture. Following that with a 333 (pronounced "*ba ba ba*") or an ice-cold Tiger Beer is practically an institution in Ho Chi Minh City. Beer will sometimes be served with a glass of ice to pour over.

The largest beer company in Vietnam is Sabeco, once state-owned but now majority-owned by a Thai beverage conglomerate. It has over 50 percent of the market, serves more than a billion liters annually, and produces the "Saigon" and "333" brands. These beers can be found almost anywhere.

International beers are quite popular as well. You can find Tiger Beer (originally a Singaporean local beer, now owned by Heineken Asia Pacific), Heineken (Dutch), Carlsberg (Danish), Sapporo (Japanese), Singha (Thai), and a few others around. There is also an emerging craft beer scene, including the Pasteur Brewing Company.

Traditional wine is not common at the Vietnamese dinner table. The warm climate in Vietnam is not conducive to storing wine for any length of time. Also, be wary of wine purchases in Vietnam as an unfortunate amount of bottle counterfeiting exists (just as in other Asian countries). Buying wine in higher-end restaurants, however, especially international ones, is as natural as anywhere else in the world. Some well-curated wine lists can be found.

If you pair wine with Vietnamese food, the Austrian Gruner-Veltliner grape variety can be a stunning match, as can off-dry Riesling, Gewürztraminer, and Sauvignon Blanc (especially Australian). The brightness of pinot noir can be a spectacular, complementary red wine for fresh Vietnamese cuisine as well, as long as it is not paired with a spicy dish.

Cognac, another vestige of Vietnam's colonial past, is quite popular in Ho Chi Minh City. You will find this brandy in many high-end bars where frequent guests buy and then keep their own bottles at the bar for future visits. It is acknowledged as a celebratory beverage. You will often hear Vietnamese refer to Cognac (and other brandies) as "wine."

The Sweetness of Dessert

Desserts in Ho Chi Minh City are underrated on the world stage. Sadly, some Vietnamese cookbooks don't even mention them. In a land where sugarcane grows abundantly, those blessed with a sweet tooth should not neglect the indulgent pleasures of the Mekong Delta.

One of the first dessert-related words of the Vietnamese language you should learn and remember is *che*, the word for "sweet soup." *Che* is an umbrella term for many different pudding- or liquid-like desserts that are served in a bowl to be eaten with a spoon. One example is *che troi nuoc*, which consists of sweet mung bean paste in a glutinous rice flour dumpling served in a sweet ginger sauce and sprinkled with toasted sesame seeds. Another is *che chuoi*, a warm banana, tapioca, and coconut milk soup. There are many other kinds of *che* to try as well, each a sweet, creative treasure of local ingredients and flavors.

Fresh fruit is quite popular as a dessert item in Ho Chi Minh City. Primarily you will see bananas, papaya, mango, and watermelon served, but other fruits are also available, depending on the season. Often, these fruits will be intricately and masterfully carved for presentation purposes before arriving at your table.

Banana sticky rice cake wrapped in a banana leaf, known as *banh chuoi*, is another classic that is frequently sold via street vendor. Fried bananas and grilled bananas slathered in a warm coconut sauce are favorites that make use of Vietnam's plentiful local banana supply. Pumpkin pudding in banana leaves is another classic.

Sticky rice with durian sauce, coconut pandan cake, and mango or papaya flan are other favorites. The lychee granita, with fresh lychees, lychee syrup, and crushed ice, takes advantage of the profusion of lychees in the region.

Vietnamese ice cream, or *kem*, can be found around town. Ho Chi Minh City isn't particularly well-known for its ice cream, not to mention that it won't last very long in the sun and may end up mostly down your sleeve. If you do insist upon giving it a shot (and it would be hard to blame you in the intense heat), go with a local fruit flavor such as mango, durian, or papaya.

Many of the sweet drinks in the *Beverage Landscape* section can be enjoyed as dessert and are the go-to option for a lot of Vietnamese. Banana and coconut candy will test the strength of your teeth if you get a chance to sample these unique, locally made delights.

All in all, the desserts of Ho Chi Minh City are a great way to finish off a local meal. They will provide for many sweet memories of your trip to Vietnam.

Banh chuoi (banana cake)

Where to Eat

Ho Chi Minh City's thrilling restaurant scene is unique, visually spectacular, and astonishingly delicious. It is among the great dining destinations of the world. Here, you will find some of the most strikingly beautiful, romantic, and elegant restaurants in all of Asia, and some of the most energetic and exciting local eateries anywhere. Bold, traditional regional flavors match polite yet spirited service. The adventuresome local cuisine showcases the beautiful convergence of where the present embraces the past, intermingling with the influence and creativity of bygone eras.

Along with the city's dynamite panorama of restaurants, the vast and far-reaching street food scene is an even greater experience for wide-eyed, hungry travelers following the smell of glowing charcoal grills and their sizzling meats and seafood. Nightly, the air pungently swirls with the fresh-herb aromas and heat of southern Vietnamese goodness. Street food can sometimes be every bit as flavorful and fresh as similar dishes in upscale restaurants, just without the ambience (and corresponding price). Missing out on the street food scene is missing out on Ho Chi Minh City.

Without a doubt, eating in Ho Chi Minh City will be a major highlight of your trip. Be sure that you experience a cross-section of the city's edible offerings in the time you have available. This will help you attain a full appreciation of the complexity and brilliance this one-of-a-kind gastronomic culture has to offer.

The first thing to understand is that the Vietnamese eat dinner early. This is because restaurants and street food vendors buy their food fresh daily and therefore need to estimate demand. In turn, customers have learned that the early bird gets the worm. Prime dinner time is usually 6 or 6:30 p.m. in many restaurants. If you risk a 7:30 p.m. or 8 p.m. dinner arrival, there is a decent chance that much of the menu will be sold out. This is less true at some of the more upscale, reservation-based establishments. However, when possible, eat early.

Another thing to be aware of is that a Vietnamese server will often stand at your table after providing menus. This is cultural and not an attempt to hurry your order or move you along. The server will usually quietly wait there until you have made decisions in an effort to provide exemplary, attentive service. He or she will answer any questions that you have while you study the selections. If you do happen to take a significant amount of time, which is ok, they may walk away to tend to another table. If a server standing at the table does make you uncomfortable, it is completely acceptable to ask them to come back in a little while, so you don't feel rushed.

As far as tipping, it is not necessarily expected at casual restaurants. Although, if you have the means, 50k to 100k dong (under $5 USD) would be greatly appreciated. In more upscale restaurants, 10 percent or so is customary. Cash tips have a far better likelihood of ending up in your server's pocket.

Many street food restaurants and casual restaurants specialize in a single dish. This is of course cost-effective for the ownership and enables the given venue to focus all efforts on that specific offering. This can result in a spectacular rendition of the particular dish, especially for the price. These single-item establishments will be easy to spot as the dish is often in the name of the restaurant, such as *Bun Bo Hue 31*. If you are interested in trying a given specialty, this is an excellent way to go.

You are encouraged to visit websites where available to learn more about a given restaurant experience, read online reviews, and obtain the various perspectives the many wonderful blogs our culinary fan peers provide about local restaurants and street food locales. Most travelers will likely have only a handful of meals while in the city. You will want to maximize your experience in a place that appeals to you and avoid any duds. This can be achieved with ample research.

The restaurant listings herein have been split into five separate categories. Note that the beautiful and upscale restaurants in Ho Chi Minh City are geared towards tourists with prices to match (similar to Western prices), but they are usually wonderful experiences and far from "touristy." This is because most Vietnamese don't have the financial means to enjoy such places, and even if they did, they probably would not pay the higher prices. Their immense knowledge of the local cuisine scene makes them less interested in a "cultural experience." This is why many of these beautiful restaurants are sometimes not crowded.

The selections below serve only as a guide. Anyone who has read online restaurant reviews is probably amazed how similar groups of people can both love and hate the same restaurant. And of course, every restaurant has its off nights and weak links, while other nights, certain individuals can help an otherwise average restaurant shine wonderfully. There is always an element of just rolling the dice. Smile, be adventurous, and enjoy experiencing one of the great cuisines emerging on the world stage.

Price Key (USD):
$ - Under $10/per person
$$ - $10-$20/per person
$$$ - $20-$50/per person
$$$$ - $50+/per person

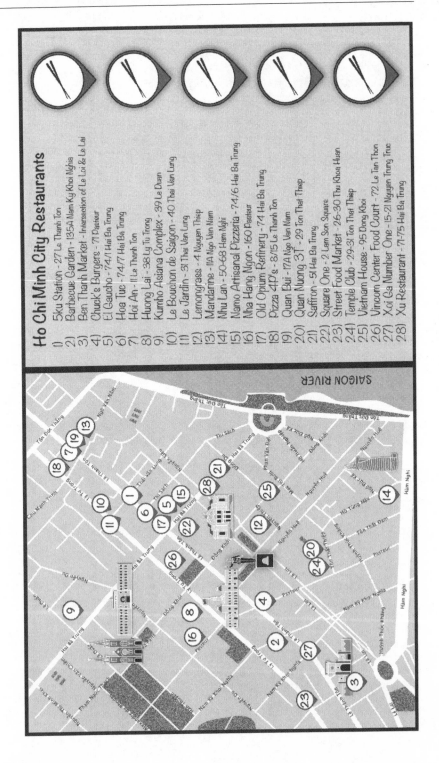

Ho Chi Minh City Restaurants

1) 5ku Station - 27 Le Thanh Ton
2) Barbecue Garden - 135A Nam Ky Khoi Nghia
3) Ben Thanh Market - Intersection of Le Loi & Le Lai
4) Chuck's Burgers - 71 Pasteur
5) El Gaucho - 74/1 Hai Ba Trung
6) Hoa Tuc - 74/7 Hai Ba Trung
7) Hoi An - 11 Le Thanh Ton
8) Huong Lai - 38 Ly Tu Trong
9) Kumho Asiana Complex - 39 Le Duan
10) Le Bouchon de Saigon - 40 Thai Van Lung
11) Le Jardin - 31 Thai Van Lung
12) Lemongrass - 4 Nguyen Thiep
13) Mandarine - 11A Ngo Van Nam
14) Nhu Lan - 50-68 Ham Nghi
15) Namo Artisanal Pizzeria - 74/6 Hai Ba Trung
16) Nha Hang Ngon - 160 Pasteur
17) Old Opium Refinery - 74 Hai Ba Trung
18) Pizza 4P's - 8/15 Le Thanh Ton
19) Quan Bui - 17A Ngo Van Nam
20) Quan Nuong 3T - 29 Ton That Thiep
21) Saffron - 51 Hai Ba Trung
22) Square One - 2 Lam Son Square
23) Street Food Market - 26-30 Thu Khoa Huan
24) Temple Club - 29-31 Ton That Thiep
25) Vietnam House - 95 Dong Khoi
26) Vincom Center Food Court - 72 Le Tan Thon
27) Xoi Ga Number One - 15-21 Nguyen Trung Truc
28) Xu Restaurant - 71-75 Hai Ba Trung

Vietnamese Upscale

$$$$ Ly Club – Named after the 11th century Vietnamese Ly dynasty that ruled for two centuries, the romantic Ly Club resides on both floors of an elegant, beautifully maintained French villa. The decoratively sculpted white walls and vibrant paintings conjure a classical ambience within the villa, where both traditional Vietnamese and creative international set and a la carte menus are professionally served. There is a solid international wine list available. Outside in the garden, there is a chic cocktail bar, ideal to visit for a drink prior to dinner, or on its own. Outside restaurant seating is also available. *08:00 – 22:00, daily.* (**www.lyclub.vn/saigon**) 143 Nam Ky Khoi Nghia (District 1) (+84 8 3930 5588)

$$$ An Vien – As many restaurants in Ho Chi Minh City are, this beautiful old Vietnamese residence-turned-restaurant is hidden down an alley, next to the Tous l'Jour pastry shop. The old villa is luxurious, peaceful, and magnificently decorated. It is ideal for a quiet, romantic evening. Attentive service provides traditional, yet creative Vietnamese cuisine with a commendable wine list to match. *07:00 – 22:00, daily.* 178A Hai Ba Trung (District 1) (+84 8 3824 3877)

$$$ Mandarine (#13) – Despite a name that frequently confuses tourists, this enchanting restaurant serves traditional Vietnamese cuisine accompanied by live entertainment (such as violins) in an elegant, refined, and intimate setting. A *mandarin* is the highest level of scholar in Vietnamese culture, a name befitting the sophisticated and splendidly decorated restaurant. It provides both set and a la carte menus with professional service in beautiful surrounds. Located down a well-known side street off Le Thanh Ton, there is also a lengthy wine list. The multi-room establishment is one of Ho Chi Minh City's finer ambiences, perfect for a wonderful evening. *11:30 – 14:00, 17:30 – 22:45, daily* (**www.orientalsaigon.com.vn/mandarine**) 11A Ngo Van Nam (District 1) (+84 8 3822 9783)

$$$ Hoi An (#7) – Around the corner on the main thoroughfare, owned and run by the same group that owns Mandarine, Hoi An is also a traditional, beautiful, teakwood restaurant that has won several awards for its cuisine and ambience. The sophisticated presentation and decor includes live traditional Vietnamese music, peacefully performed while you dine. The restaurant's signature dish is *cao lau*, which originates from the beautiful city of Hoi An in central Vietnam. Hoi An is near Hue, the imperial city, from where the restaurant elegantly presents many of central Vietnam's traditional dishes. *11:30 – 14:00, 17:30 – 22:45, daily* (**www.orientalsaigon.com.vn/hoian**) 11 Le Thanh Ton (District 1) (+84 8 3823 7694)

$$$ Temple Club (#24) – This restaurant exists in a former guest house to the nearby Hindu temple that has existed across the street since the 1880s. The fashionable, throwback Temple Club serves Vietnamese cuisine with Chinese, Khmer, Indian, and French influences, a reflection of the city's culinary history. Located on the second floor with a candle-lit staircase leading the way, it can be a little difficult to find. Still, it is a romantic, relaxing, and memorable gastronomic experience. The seafood with tamarind sauce and steamed coconut shrimp are excellent choices. There are multiple dining rooms, including a fashionable colonial-style cocktail bar to enjoy before or after dinner. *12:00 – 24:00, daily* (**www.templeclub.com.vn**) 29-31 Ton That Thiep (District 1) (+84 8 3829 9244)

$$$ Trinh Restaurant – In a vintage, wonderfully decorated villa tucked down an alley is the delightful Trinh Restaurant. The restaurant is an homage to Vietnam War-era musician Trinh Cong Son, who passed away in 2001 (see the *Film, Literature, and Music* section). He was one of the most talented composers of his time. His beautiful guitar-based music was long a favorite of many Vietnamese. You will feel like you are having an elegantly prepared meal in the musician's living room while dining here. The cuisine consists of the imperial dishes of Hue and central Vietnam politely served in the tranquility of the dining room with Son's music softly playing in the background. *08:00 – 22:00, daily* (**www.facebook.com/trinhrestaurantcafe**) 41/5 Pham Ngoc Thach (District 3) (+84 8 3829 7437)

$$$ Tib – Found down a narrow, lantern-lined lane, Tib is another classy restaurant from the same owner of Trinh Restaurant. It has been open since 1993. Here, waitresses in traditional *ao dai* gowns serve the imperial cuisine of Hue and central Vietnam while the suit-and-tie floor manager oversees. The hardwood-themed decor inside is relaxing and lovingly adorned with vases and other traditional Vietnamese art. The wine list is extensive, and the restaurant features indoor and outdoor seating options. US President George W. Bush and Australian Prime Minister John Howard have dined here. The original location is near downtown on Hai Ba Trung Street, however there is now a second location in the farther-out suburban district of Phu My Hung in District 7. There is also a vegetarian version of the restaurant nearby worth discovering. *11:00 – 14:00, 17:00 – 22:00, daily* (**tibrestaurant.com.vn**) 187 Ter, Hai Ba Trung (District 3) (+84 8 3829 7242)

$$$$ Nam Phan – Located in a grand, beautifully appointed four-story villa and one of several "luxury" restaurants of the Khai silk family, Nam Phan provides European prestige and classical, high-browed ambience with marble floors, candles, lovely furniture, and stone-carved walls. This is all set against a quiet background of classical music. Its upscale, traditional Vietnamese cuisine with multiple set menus at different price points is delivered with formal service. Tables are spread well apart for comfort and privacy, although there can be celebrations or large business dinners occurring from time to time in the posh setting. *10:30 – 14:00, 17:00 – 22:00, daily* (**www.khaisilkcorp.com/restaurants/namphan**) 34 Vo Van Tan (District 3) (+84 8 3933 3636)

$$$ Cuc Gach Quan – Set in a quiet neighborhood in a converted, multi-floored, French colonial house reminiscent of the 1970s, rustic "country" Vietnamese cuisine inspired by the owner's grandmother is cozily and intimately presented. The oasis-like pond, antiques, flowers, and other botanical delights throughout provide for a tranquil residence feel to accompany the charmingly prepared cuisine. There is a long menu of traditional favorites available in this nostalgic setting. Sometimes this restaurant is referred to locally as "The Architect" in reference to Vietnamese architect-owner Tran Binh who designed the villa's conversion to the restaurant. There is a second restaurant available across the street that you might be directed to if Cuc Gach Quan is full. It has a similar menu. *09:00 – 23:00, daily* (**www.cucgachquan.com.vn**) 10 Dang Tat (District 1) (+84 8 3848 0144)

$$$ Xu (#28) – In the modern category of upscale Ho Chi Minh City restaurants, Xu boasts of see-and-be-seen crowds dining on creative, modern interpretations of Vietnamese cuisine prepared with local ingredients. One of the more popular clubs in town is on the first floor while the Xu lounge and restaurant sits up top in earshot on the second floor. Friendly service and a sophisticated wine and cocktail menu accompany the contemporary, evocative set menus (a la carte also available). *11:30 – 24:00, daily* (**www.xusaigon.com**) 71-75 Hai Ba Trung (District 1) (+84 8 3824 8468)

Additional Vietnamese

$$ Lemongrass (#12) – A traveler's favorite since 1996, this restaurant is situated downtown on a relatively quiet street in a French villa setting. It offers excellent, traditional southern Vietnamese dishes for both lunch and dinner. Classics such as clay pot entrees, lemongrass-scented poultry and beef, curry, and seafood dishes including sea bass, lobster, and crab are served in a three-story quaint, colonial structure. *10:00 – 22:30, daily* (**www.lemongrasssaigon.com**) 4 Nguyen Thiep (District 1) (+84 8 3822 0496)

$$ Hoa Tuc (#6) – Offering excellent cooking classes, Hoa Tuc also serves well-presented contemporary Vietnamese dishes both inside and outside underneath its charming Paris Metro-inspired roof. It is located in the garden courtyard of the old colonial Opium Refinery (Hoa Tuc means "poppy" in Vietnamese) off Hai Ba Trung Street within a community of other restaurants. It's a pleasing location on a warm evening to enjoy tantalizing dishes such as shrimp and papaya coconut pancakes, barbecued sea bass with lemongrass, barbecued turmeric mackerel in a banana leaf, the classic *bo la lot* (lemongrass beef grilled in betel leaves), or a braised duck leg in ginger sauce. *11:00 – 23:00, daily* (**www.hoatuc.com**) 74/7 Hai Ba Trung (District 1) (+84 8 3825 1676)

$$ Quan Bui (#19) – Authentic Vietnamese dishes are served in a pleasingly decorated, cozy four-story villa in the old French Quarter on Ngo Van Nam Street, including a garden rooftop setting. Classic dishes include braised seafood, boiled pork with salted white eggplant, steamed local breed chicken, and several beautifully presented "Quan Bui" signature dishes. *08:00 – 23:00, daily* (**https://quan-bui.com**) 17A Ngo Van Nam (District 1) (+84 9 1400 8835)

$$ Nha Hang Ngon (#16) – With an open-air banana-tree-in-a-French-villa setting, this canary-yellow-painted restaurant enables diners to wander and discover various street-style cuisine stations and determine what looks appetizing before ordering from one's table. The name of the restaurant translates to "restaurant tastes good," which is highly accurate. Try classics such as *chao tom* (shrimp skewered on sugarcane, and then rolled in rice paper with fresh vegetables); lobster with salt, pepper, chili, and lime juice; or pork and rice noodle spring rolls, all complemented with ice-cold Vietnamese suds. Popular with tourists and locals, be sure to go early as the best, freshest dishes can disappear quickly. *07:00 – 22:00, daily* (**www.quananngon.com**) 160 Pasteur (District 1) (+84 8 3827 7131)

$$ Com Nieu Sai Gon – Famous for its crispy, clay pot-breaking smashed rice that gets tossed around by the service staff and for multiple Anthony Bourdain visits for television, this popular, buzzing, high energy restaurant has several hundred regional specialties on its menu. It is a top spot for locals too, especially for lunch. *09:00 – 23:00, daily* 19 Tu Xuong (District 3) (+84 8 3932 6388)

$$ Vietnam House (#25) – Located in yet another former French colonial villa, this cozy downtown restaurant on busy Dong Khoi Street has been serving traditional Vietnamese dishes for years. The pineapple fried rice, summer rolls, basa fish, and famous whole Gorami fish (that you wrap yourself in rice paper with rice noodles served with fresh and pickled vegetables) are all first-rate choices. *10:00 – 23:00, daily* (**www.vietnamhousesaigon.com**) 95 Dong Khoi (District 1) (+84 8 3829 1623)

$$$ Marina – At this seafood establishment, select your live seafood (crab, lobster, fish, tiger prawns, and more) from the various water tanks in the back for the chefs to grill and elegantly prepare. You can have a pleasant dining experience inside or outside in a classic Vietnamese ambience. There is frequently live, local music in the outside dining area. *11:00 – 22:00, daily*
(**mariasaigon.com.vn**) 172C Nguyen Dinh Chieu (District 3) (+84 8 3930 2379)

$$$ Gao – With glowing lanterns in its outdoor dining area (a nifty perch to watch the city go by), this former mansion with the white horse out front is a great spot to enjoy some creative Vietnamese dishes. Try the red rice and beans in bamboo or the chargrilled beef wrapped in a banana leaf. *07:00 – 22:00, daily*
33 Le Quy Don (District 3) (+84 8 3932 6632)

$$ Viet Village – You will likely need a taxi from downtown as it is approximately ten blocks away to visit this cozy, rustic little "village" restaurant. Elegantly presented traditional Vietnamese food is served. There is a nostalgic display of old Vietnamese bicycles within the restaurant. *10:00 – 22:00, daily* (**www.vietvillage.com.vn**) 15 Dinh Tien Hoang (District 1) (+84 8 3911 7261)

$$ Binh Quoi 1 & 2 – Quite a respectable distance from District 1, a visit to Binh Quoi and its Mekong River-like grounds can make for a wonderful weekend evening among locals (and a handful of Western tourists). The multi-station buffet style restaurant enables going from station to station loading up plates with every beautiful dish that you lay eyes upon. This is of course after you have filled your mobile device with pictures (Binh Quoi 2 being the more picturesque) from the captivating riverside grounds. Accompanied by live traditional Vietnamese music performances, the setting is alongside a canal with old bridges and floating lanterns just off the Saigon River. The trip for an outdoor weekend dinner of traditional Vietnamese dishes can be well worth the travel time of twenty minutes from the city center. Binh Quoi 1 is another few minutes' drive farther out than Binh Quoi 2. *Saturday and Sunday evenings.* (**www.binhquoiresort.com.vn**) 1147 Duong Binh Quoi (Binh Tanh District) (+84 8 5566 020)

$$ Huong Lai (#8) – This socially conscious restaurant provides fantastic French and Vietnamese cuisine served up an old staircase in a quaint little Southeast Asian colonial-style oasis. Lunch and dinner is served in a high ceiling second floor loft away from the busy street noise below. Some of the kitchen staff and the service staff are former street kids, poor children, and orphans, perhaps on their way to future Michelin stars. These hard workers are learning on the job and given a place to stay. This is good food for a good cause, served in a polite setting. *12:00 – 14:00, 18:00 – 21:00, daily* (**www.huonglai2001saigon.com**) 38 Ly Tu Trong (District 1) (+84 8 3822 6814)

Street Food Experiences

In and around **Ben Thanh Market** (#3, also see *Major Sights*), there are several food vendor stalls selling many different traditional Vietnamese dishes. You'll find flavorful noodle dishes, shrimp and pork summer rolls, hot and spicy soups, and many different desserts and sweet soups (for which the stall *Be Che* is a great choice). Walk around and visit the various vendors until you see something that looks potentially pleasing. Be adventurous. Also, around the block surrounding the market, there are many street vendors with their soup cauldrons and charcoal grills selling traditional dishes, cash-only of course. These are available throughout most of the day, especially on Phan Boi Chau Street. During the night market on these same streets, several seafood and traditional Vietnamese pop-up restaurants appear lighting up the sky with the flames of their grills, several of which are great choices for a sit-down dinner. Look for places with lots of people, as the volume turnover keeps the ingredients fresh. *06:00 – 18:00, daily (night market, late)* Intersection of Le Loi & Le Lai (District 1)

$ Street Food Market (#23) – Opened in December of 2015 and a couple of blocks walk from the original Ben Thanh Market, the new hawker-style "Ben Thanh Street Food Market" is a covered collection of street vendors with a variety of mostly traditional Vietnamese food. There are additionally some other Asian offerings, such as Thai. Wander from vendor to vendor until you find something desirable. Covered picnic table seating is available. *06:00 – 24:00, daily* 26-30 Thu Khoa Huan (District 1) (+84 9 0688 1707)

$$ 5ku Station (#1) – At this energetic, happening Vietnamese do-it-yourself charcoal barbecue firehouse, you can cook various marinated meats and vegetables on your personal grill at a wooden table and swill ice-cold Tiger beer or the local 333. Portions of the menu are prepared in back by the chefs if you prefer to minimize self-cooking or try some of the more exotic dishes. Open air, high energy, and filled with tourists, expats, and locals alike, it is open quite late, stays hot and tasty, and provides endless revelry and fun. *16:00 – 04:00, daily* (**www.facebook.com/5kuStation**) 27 Le Thanh Ton (District 1) (+84 9 0777 5487)

$$ Quan Nuong 3T (#20) – This is another high-energy do-it-yourself barbecue spot on the second-floor roof where many locals celebrate life with a metal-topped grill at every table. The skewered prawns may still be kicking when they arrive at your table, so expect freshness. The squid and marinated wild boar are also sensational, fiery favorites. *17:00 – 23:00, daily* 29 Ton That Thiep (District 1) (+84 9 0835 7530)

$ Bun Bo Hue 31 – This is a great street spot to try the spicy, Hue imperial soup classic *bun bo Hue*. Be sure to get the optional, paired meat by pointing to the *cha lua* (ham-like steamed pork loaf in banana leaf wrappers) and add them to the fragrant soup. They are usually available on the main cart up front. *06:00 – 21:00, daily* 31 Mac Dinh Chi (District 1) (+84 8 3827 7257)

$ The Lunch Lady – Another street food locale made famous by travel shows, this hard-to-find outside corner spot serves a different noodle soup every day, usually with fresh *goi cuon* summer rolls or *cha gio* spring rolls. Find a little red or blue open chair, sit down and the staff will take superb care of you. The motherly star of the show stirs a flavorful cauldron of a traditional bubbling soup every hot afternoon, but so it goes in the heat of Ho Chi Minh City (soup keeps locals hydrated). The scene can be spectacular as the sweat drips off the brows of each patron. It's down a little side street off Hoang Sa Street. *10:30 – 15:30, daily* 23 Hoang Sa (District 1)

$ Cau Ba Quan – This street-side eatery sells fresh, grilled-on-the-sidewalk seafood from Phu Quoc island and provides some novel twists on Vietnamese cuisine. Owner Nickie Tran spent fifteen years living in the US. Her English is solid, and she can help with menu questions and suggestions if she is around. *10:00 – 24:00, daily* (**www.facebook.com/caubaquan82**) 80-82 Mac Dinh Chi (District 1) (+84 9 0988 5033)

$ Nhu Lan (#14) – Known for its classic *banh mi* sandwiches and its bakery, this 24-hour, well-stocked, mouth-watering sidewalk joint has been here since 1968. It serves many traditional Vietnamese dishes for eating in the restaurant, but just as often the delights are ordered "to go." *24 hours, daily* 50-68 Ham Nghi (District 1) (+84 8 8292 970)

$ Pho Le – A bit far from the City Center in District 5, Pho Le is argued by many to have some of the best southern-style *pho* in Ho Chi Minh City. You will find many locals here slurping away at noodles with a sweet, sour, fragrant broth. *06:00 – 01:00, daily* 413-415 Nguyen Trai (District 5)

$ Pho Quynh – In Pham Ngu Lao, this is another contender for top street *pho* in the city. *24 hours, daily* 323 Pham Ngu Lao (District 1) (+84 8 3837 6310)

$ Pho Hoa – And yet another vying for best *pho* in the city. *07:00 – 23:00, daily* 260C Pasteur (District 1) (+84 8 3829 7943).

$$ BBQ Saigon Night – On Bui Vien Street in the backpacker's district, the seating is a little uncomfortable (and you may even choose to eat on the steps). Simply point at what's fresh on the cart and soon it will be delivered to you smoking from the barbecue grill. Skewered chicken, beef, shrimp, squid, and vegetables in all sorts of combinations are on offer. *18:00 – 24:00, daily* 198/4 Bui Vien (District 1) (+84 9 0823 0721)

$ Bun Cha – Also on Bui Vien Street, this little spot is famous for its Hanoi-style grilled pork and noodle dishes. *12:00 – 14:00, 17:30 – 22:00, daily* 145 Bui Vien (District 1) (+84 8 3837 3474)

$ Xoi Ga Number One (#27) – A block from Ben Thanh Market, this chicken and sticky rice favorite grew from a tiny little station to one of the best street food locales in the city. It now spans a couple of store-fronts. The noodles are warm and delicious here as well. *07:00 – 20:30, daily* (**www.xoiganumberone.com**) 15-21 Nguyen Trung Truc (District 1) (+84 8 3825 0818)

$$ Oc Dao – A backstreet snail-fest, this hard-to-find locals' spot consists of a large covered courtyard and many different snail dishes, shellfish, and other seafood grilled on an open charcoal flame. It is inexpensive, and a great place for a truly local culinary experience, all of which to wash down with some ice-cold local beer. With usually hundreds of people here, it can be quite a festive environment. Many taxi drivers will know the location, but if you try to find it on your own, bring a detailed map and best of luck to you, as very little English is spoken in these back-street parts, including at the restaurant. 212/C79 Nguyen Trai (District 1) *10:00 – 23:00, daily*

$ Mon Hue – A chain restaurant having little charm and with several locations in the city, it is a worthwhile opportunity to try some Hue specialties without the price tag of some of the more upscale establishments. (**www.nhahangmonhue.vn**) There are nearly thirty locations in Ho Chi Minh City, including one near Ben Thanh Market (District 1). *06:00 – 23:00, daily*

An example of street food you can find around Ho Chi Minh City

International Upscale

$$$$ La Villa (French) – A significant distance from the city center in District 2, La Villa is a stately, poolside French mansion where French haute cuisine is delightfully presented in a *belle époque*-like setting. Opened by French Chef Thierry in 2010, who has trained and worked at Michelin-starred restaurants in France and London, you can find French classics such as Brittany lobster bisque, foie gras, and black truffle dishes here. Indoor and outdoor seating is accommodated with set menus available. There is a thoughtful wine list developed from many French grape-growing regions, especially Bordeaux, and a handful of New World wines. *11:45 – 13:30, 18:30 – 21:30, Monday-Saturday* (**www.lavilla-restaurant.com.vn**) 14 Ngo Quang Huy (District 2) (+84 9 0771 9879)

$$$$ Au Manoir De Khai (French) – Refined and opulent in its classical, grandiose ambience, the hundred-year-old mansion provides an elegant haute cuisine dining experience both inside and outside the mansion. This includes tuxedoed waiters, an extensive wine list, and old-world cheese carts. The restaurant could easily be found in the stylish neighborhood of St. Germain, Paris. With the same owners as Nam Phan in the upscale Vietnamese section, the menu is entirely French with prices to match. *18:00 – 22:00, daily* (**www.khaisilkcorp.com/restaurants/aumanoirdekhai**) 251 Dien Bien Phu (District 3) (+84 8 3930 3394)

$$$$ Square One (#22, Vietnamese and Western) – Located in the newly renovated Park Hyatt Saigon, Square One is a modern, stylish restaurant with five separate dining areas (including an outdoor terrace). The professional staff serves multiple cuts of steak, fresh seafood such as Nha Trang lobster, and other exquisitely prepared Western dishes. There are also Vietnamese menu items such as several clay pot dishes and a wagyu beef *pho*. In addition to tropical cocktails, there is an immense wine list with over twelve hundred bottles on display. *11:30 – 14:30, 18:00 – 22:30, daily* (**www.saigon.park.hyattrestaurants.com/squareOne/default-en.html**) 2 Lam Son Square (District 1) (+84 8 3824 1234)

$$$$ The Deck (Western-style Modern Pan-Asian) – In District 2, twenty minutes by hired car from downtown Ho Chi Minh City, you also have the option of scheduling a boat pickup and drop-off for the trendy restaurant (boat is pricey, schedule in advance), as it is situated on the edge of the Saigon River. A torch-lit courtyard lounge setting is appealing for a drink or two before or after dinner. Eclectic menu options include dishes such as Japanese scallops, duck breast with cashew nuts and watermelon, foie gras dumplings, and Angus ribeye. *08:00 – 24:00, daily* (**www.thedecksaigon.com**) 38 Nguyen U Di (District 2) (+84 8 3744 6632)

$$$ Shri (Western) – On top of the Centec building, this modern Western-style restaurant and lounge with terrace seating provides spectacular panoramic views overlooking the downtown skyline. It is a chic, yet relaxed, intimate setting nestled in the metropolitan sky. Professionally presented dishes are all Western with a wine list and cocktails to pair. *10:30 – 24:00, daily* (**www.shri.vn**) 72-74 Nguyen Thi Minh Khai, Centec Building (District 3) (+84 8 3827 9633)

$$$ El Gaucho (#5, Argentinian) – El Gaucho is an Argentinian-style steakhouse serving cuts of meat from Australia and the US, rather than from the Pampas in South America. The restaurant offers classic ribeye, filets, and sirloins fit for any modern-day cowboy regardless if from Argentina, Vietnam, or elsewhere. Items from the wine list with New and Old-World selections can also be purchased from the restaurant at a discount to take away. Salads, beef carpaccio, chorizo, and the eponymous El Gaucho platter appetizer can ensure a filling meal. The bar and dining room make for a gratifying South American-style evening. *11:00 – 24:00, daily* (**vn.elgaucho.asia**) 74/1 Hai Ba Trung (District 1) (+84 8 3827 2090)

$$$$ Trois Gourmand (French) – One of the finest French restaurants in Ho Chi Minh City, the Chef-owner is also a sommelier, providing one of the best curated French wine lists in town, including labels from Bordeaux, Burgundy, the Loire Valley, Beaujolais, the Rhone Valley, and the Southwest of France. Within the villa's pleasant dining room or on the beautiful poolside outdoor terrace, you will find truffles and foie gras to pair with beef, seafood, and other French classics, and also a multi-course degustation menu. *11:00 – 14:00, 18:00 – 21:30, Tuesday-Sunday* (**www.3gourmandsaigon.com.vn**) 39 Tran Ngoc Dien (District 2) (+84 8 3744 4585)

$$$ Le Bordeaux (French) – A little ways out from the city center but on the downtown side of the Saigon River, Le Bordeaux is another excellent French option. French-trained Chef Phuc returned to Vietnam over twenty years ago and delivers an adventure in French gastronomy in an impeccably European-decorated setting. Rack of lamb, scallops, pheasant, and duck are frequent options. The restaurant can be difficult to find. It might be best to arrange a taxi with the restaurant or your hotel to get there. *11:30 – 13:30, 18:30 – 22:00, Monday-Saturday* (**www.restaurantlebordeaux.com**) 72 Duong D2 (District Binh Thanh) (+84 8 3899 9831)

$$$ Ocean Palace (Chinese) – A large, lavish dining hall near the zoo and botanical gardens, the refined restaurant has fresh seafood in tanks and an attentive, professional staff. This is an impressive setting for Chinese classics such as Beijing duck and dim sum. Many additional dishes are available on weekends. *09:00 – 23:00, daily* (**www.facebook.com/oceanpalacevietnam**) 2 Le Duan (District 1) (+84 8 3911 8822)

International Casual

$$ Pizza 4P's (#18) – This popular Neapolitan-style pizza restaurant with Japanese pizza master ownership serves up oven-baked pies, including Italian classics such as the Margherita. The cheese is made daily in Dalat. There are also some local twists to the menu, including the "Vietnamese Four Flower Pizza." Arrive early for lunch or make a reservation, as it is often full. It is down an alley and to the left off Le Thanh Ton Street. As of September 2016, there is a second location near Ben Thanh Market at 8 Thu Khoa Huan Street, with a few more to open (check the Website). *10:00 – 22:30, daily* (**www.pizza4ps.com**) 8/15 Le Thanh Ton (District 1) (+84 12 0789 4444)

$$ Namo Restaurant and Pizzeria (#15) – This pizzeria is run by a couple of Italian guys. You might discover them inside joyfully drinking glasses of Barolo wine while flipping dough. There are multiple floors, and a large Neapolitan pizza oven in the window firing out classic Italian specialties. *11:00 – 23:00, daily* (**www.namorestaurant.com**) 74/6 Hai Ba Trung (District 1) (+84 8 3822 7988)

$$ Saffron (#21) – This establishment offers Mediterranean fare in a cozy brick-walled restaurant, including dishes from Spain, Italy, Greece, North Africa, and the Middle East. *11:00 – 23:00, daily* (**www.saffronvietnam.com**) 51 Hai Ba Trung (District 1) (+84 8 3824 8358)

$$ Le Jardin (#11) – Le Jardin provides a rustic French bistro-style experience in a terrace garden atmosphere offering some tranquility away from the madness of the city. *11:00 – 23:00, Monday-Saturday* 31 Thai Van Lung (District 1) (+84 8 3825 8465)

$$ Barbecue Garden (#2) – Outdoor, garden-style, do-it-yourself barbecue. There are two locations of this restaurant that are more family friendly than the other barbecue choices listed in this book. Here, they offer Vietnamese classics such as skewered tiger prawns, but also provide menu choices from a global range of barbecue styles, including Indonesian, Thai, Australian, and more. *11:00 – 23:00, daily* (**www.barbecuegarden.vn**) 135A Nam Ky Khoi Nghia (District 1) (+84 8 3823 3340)

$$ Sushi Rei – Excellent Japanese *omakase* with expertly cut and seasoned sushi served in a cool, stylish, and modern environment. All products in use are imported from Japan. *11:30 – 14:00 (Wednesday, Thursday, weekends), 17:30 – 23:00, Tuesday-Sunday* 10E1 Nguyen Thi Minh Khai (District 1) (+84 126 442 4653)

$$$ Noir – Capitalizing on the global trend of "dining in the dark" and using senses other than your vision for a different kind of culinary experience, this place has been a hit locally. *11:30 – 14:30, 17:30 – 23:00, daily* (**www.noirdininginthedark.com**) 178 Hai Ba Trung (District 1) (+84 9 8663 2525)

$ Chuck's Burgers (#4) – If you suddenly crave an American-style burger, make a beeline for Chuck's. Chuck is Vietnamese, but he has lived a total of thirty years in New York and Los Angeles. Your burgers are made to order, and are some of the best anywhere, not just Vietnam. You can try local craft beer from the Pasteur Street Brewing Company here (one of three locations). *10:00 – 22:00, daily* (**www.cburgers.com**) 71 Pasteur (District 1) (+84 9 0211 9530)

$$ TNT BBQ – Recently opened, this is a quaint American-style open-flame barbecue restaurant with great sauce, ribs, brisket, poultry, french fries, baked beans, cornbread and coleslaw. *11:00 – 22:00, daily* (**www.facebook.com/tntbbqvietnam**) 1-3 Dang Tran Con (District 1) (+84 16 6666 7858)

$$ Old Opium Refinery courtyard restaurants (#17) – In the same location as Hoa Tuc, the courtyard of this old, colonial-era opium factory and refinery hosts several restaurants, including Jaspa's, Delices, The Refinery (**www.therefinerysaigon.com**), Cava (Cage Bar & Lounge) (**www.facebook.com/cavasaigon1**), and Beirut Garden (with nightly Middle Eastern dance). 74 Hai Ba Trung (District 1)

$$ mPlaza Saigon Complex (#9) – Part of the Intercontinental Asian hotel, this complex has over seventeen different international restaurants, including Thai, Singaporean (live seafood tanks), Italian, Japanese, German, and American. There are also Starbucks and Coffee Bean and Tea Leaf locations. 39 Le Duan at Hai Ba Trung (District 1)

$ Vincom Center Food Court – This Pan-Asian collection of mostly regional chain restaurants is down a few escalator flights in the basement of the Vincom Center shopping complex off Dong Khoi Street. The location can make for a comfortable, indoor lunch break from the blazing sun if you are looking for some casual and reasonably inexpensive food with several choices in air-conditioned space. *10:00 – 22:00, daily* 72 Le Tan Thon (District 1)

In Ho Chi Minh City During Tet?

If you happen to be in town during the *Tet* holiday, it can be both a bonus and a negative depending on your perspective. Tet is the Vietnamese Lunar New Year holiday that celebrates the arrival of spring. The actual date varies each year and is based on the Chinese lunar calendar (although at times the actual New Year celebration can be on slightly different days than China's celebratory period), so it ordinarily falls in late January or in February. This is the most important holiday for the Vietnamese and an exciting time to be in Ho Chi Minh City.

The week or so leading up to Tet is a busy, hectic time as shopping, mass-decoration, and the city buzz in general is similar to that of the frenetic time leading up to Christmas in the Western world. Special holiday-only foods such as *banh chung* are available during this time, and you will see a large number of people having their picture taken around town in their traditional *ao dai* clothing. You will see many vendors selling intricately carved lunar-themed watermelons and the yellow-flowered *hoa mai* trees that the Vietnamese keep in their respective houses during the festive holiday period.

When the three days of Tet occur, the first day of which is the actual New Year's Day (don't miss the fireworks over the Saigon River), things can get quiet in the city. Most businesses and tourist attractions are closed as many city residents are at home with their families. Many others have returned to the countryside to spend the holidays in their hometowns. However, many Western restaurants remain open.

Worth witnessing, the pedestrian Nguyen Hue Boulevard is transformed into "Flower Street" and is a spectacular collection of flower-made art displays. The display extends several blocks and can be quite a bustling scene. Enjoyable live performances rock the park near Ben Thanh Market in the evenings if you find yourself here at the same time as the festivities.

During this family holiday period, many children and elderly people receive red envelopes with money in them from family members. All debts are supposed to be paid off by this time and any negative energy from the past year is to be shed. Also, the Vietnamese believe that the first person you see in the new year (after midnight of New Year's Eve) will set the tone of fortune for the year. Therefore, they desire that this first person should be a person of character. Do not visit local Vietnamese on the first day of a new year if you have not been invited.

The downside of being in the city during Tet is the daytime quiet—probably not what you came to experience. As most business and tourist locations will be shut down, for as long as a week or so, this might also be a time to visit other nearby non-Vietnam locations such as Bangkok or Siem Reap if you were intending to do so as part of your trip. They are not in a period of celebration during Tet (Thailand and Cambodia normally celebrate the new year in April). Also, locals claim that for a few days after Tet, food served in restaurants can be frozen or not as fresh, as it takes a couple of days for the food distribution network to rev up again post-holiday.

Chuc Mung Nam Moi! (Happy New Year!)

Fireworks at nightfall during Tet

Coffee Shop Culture

One of the more exciting characteristics of Ho Chi Minh City is its thriving and energetic coffee culture. Most people are unaware that Vietnam is the second largest coffee producer in the world behind Brazil. Coffee is one of Vietnam's more important agricultural export products, providing income to more than two million Vietnamese throughout mostly rural Vietnam. It had an estimated $4.5 billion USD market in 2016, representing nearly 2-3% of the national GDP.

Most of the coffee beans are grown in the Central Highlands region of Vietnam because of the favorable climatic conditions that exist there. The coffee beans grown are primarily of the *Robusta* variety, with the more esteemed *Arabica* beans currently constituting only around 5-7% of the crop. This is changing as more and more cultivators are looking towards the *Arabica* variety because of its quality and international appeal, and its share of the total output should increase over time.

In Ho Chi Minh City, because of the hot climate, iced coffee is a local favorite. It will usually be served with a sweetened, condensed, thick milk concoction. When coffee was introduced by the French in the 1800s, fresh milk was not widely available, and the sweetened condensed milk has since stuck as a popular way to consume Vietnamese coffee, especially with darker roasts.

You will mostly see Vietnamese coffee served with a tiny coffee pot and a miniature filter sitting on top of the cup. After five to ten minutes of brewing, the coffee will have dripped from the filter into the cup, which usually has the sweetened, condensed milk layer on the bottom, along with ice if a cold version is preferred. Once the dripping has finished, stir and drink!

While in cafes, the Vietnamese will spend a lot of time conversing socially before they drink any of their coffee in front of them. Not only does this patience ensure that all of the brewed coffee has dripped into the cup, but also meeting for coffee is a meaningful social event for the Vietnamese. It might be thought rude, depending on the situation, to quickly consume one's coffee beverage before it has even finished dripping or immediately after. The Vietnamese are far less likely than Westerners to order multiple cups of coffee. The one cup is to be savored and enjoyed.

Here are some different coffee types:

ca phe (ka fay) - coffee
ca phe sua (ka fay soo-uh) - coffee with milk
ca phe sua da (ka fay soo-uh dah) - iced coffee with milk
ca phe phin (ka fay feen) - drip coffee

You may also see the famous "weasel" coffee on offer in some establishments, including for sale within Ben Thanh Market. Historically, this type of coffee was brewed after esteemed beans had been "passed" by weasels who had eaten them, as peasants followed the weasels around collecting these undigested beans. These are beans that had originated from the expensive supply of colonial socialites. The enzymes from the weasel's digestive system added an incredible richness to the flavor of the coffee made from such beans (after the beans were washed of course), and they became a notoriously expensive delicacy in colonial France.

Sometimes, actual weasels may still be used (and a cup may set you back $20-$50 USD). Alternatively, a chemical is now added to the beans to create a similar effect. The resulting coffee from these weasel-enhanced beans is much richer than standard coffee, giving it an oily, chocolate-like taste that is a great match for the sweetened, condensed milk commonly found throughout Vietnam.

You can find coffee beans to purchase and take home by the kilogram in various coffee shops and for sale in markets around town such as Ben Thanh Market.

One of the benefits of the expanding coffee industry is the surprising, unique, and exciting coffee shop culture it has brought to Ho Chi Minh City. Fashionable, nostalgic, and beautifully designed and decorated coffee shops now exist throughout the city. A trip to Ho Chi Minh City without visiting a least a couple of these cafes would be a significant gap in your travel experience.

Not only a great gathering ritual for locals and tourists, a visit to a Vietnamese coffee shop is an event of substantial importance for locals. You will find people dressed up with family, on dates, or conducting business at various coffee shops around town. "Going out" for an evening often consists of visits to cozy, music-filled coffee venues. This particular scene in Ho Chi Minh City is an unexpected, fun, and comfortable way to escape the hustle and bustle of city life at all times of the day.

Here are some of the better-known coffee shops and cafes in the city:

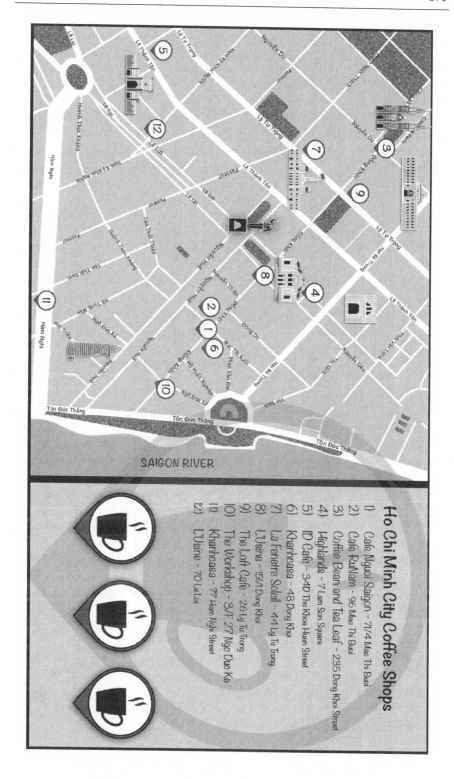

Ho Chi Minh City Coffee Shops

1) Cafe Nguoi Saigon - 71/4 Mac Thi Buoi
2) Cafe RuNam - 96 Mac Thi Buoi
3) Coffee Bean and Tea Leaf - 235 Dong Khoi Street
4) Highlands - 7 Lam Son Square
5) ID Cafe - 34D Thu Khoa Huan Street
6) Khanhcasa - 48 Dong Khoi
7) La Fenetre Soleil - 44 Ly Tu Trong
8) L'Usine - 151/1 Dong Khoi
9) The Loft Cafe - 26 Ly Tu Trong
10) The Workshop - 3/F 27 Ngo Duc Ke
11) Khanhcasa - 77 Ham Nghi Street
12) L'Usine - 70 Le Loi

The Workshop (#10) – Up two flights of stairs near Dong Khoi Street, The Workshop is one of the more polished cafes in town. It has a modern industrial feel and attracts younger ambitious types. It has an abundance of space, its own coffee bean roaster, and nifty antique glass espresso machines. With its glass-enclosed board room, the venue has the semblance of a Silicon Valley-style coffee shop transplanted to Ho Chi Minh City. There is a collection of specialty coffees and the edible offerings are mostly Western. *08:00 – 21:00, daily* (**www.facebook.com/the.workshop.coffee**) 3/F 27 Ngo Duc Ke (District 1) (+84 8 3824 6801)

The Loft Café (#9) – Another urban coffee shop, The Loft has a Somerset Maugham, *Gentleman-in-the-Parlour* feel. The classic space could easily exist in Seattle or Melbourne. It has the white walls of colonial Saigon, a giant window clock, and a light-bulbed logo behind the bar. There are tables and some restful couches to go along with the Western food menu, an ideal setting for you and your laptop. This is one of two locations (the second is at 95 Pasteur). *08:00 – 22:30, daily* (**www.theloft.vn**) 26 Ly Tu Trong (District 1) (+84 8 6682 5082)

La Fenetre Soleil (#7) – This lunchtime and evening music bar is a coffee shop by day that also serves Indonesian food. Hidden up rickety stairs with a classic French Indochinese elegance, there is a large white piano and a drum set on one side attesting to its musical soul. This posh former apartment residence has exposed brick walls, a chandelier, and charming ceiling fans. While mornings and afternoons are ideal for coffee, there is a large menu inscribed on a mirror boasting of cocktails in the evening. There is live piano entertainment for lunch and live music most nights, including the Sunday night "jam session." Evenings are also ideal for romantically sharing a bottle of wine. *09:30 – 24:00 Monday-Wednesday, until 01:00+ others, daily* (**www.facebook.com/lafenetre.soleil.3**) 44 Ly Tu Trong (District 1) (+84 8 3824 5994).

L'Usine (#8, #12) – L'Usine is a clothing shop and cafe founded by expatriates on stylish Dong Khoi Street. There are lighter European lunch items and desserts available. There is a second location on Le

Loi Street and a third on Le Thanh Ton Street. There is classic men's wear, women's wear, and a handful of curiosities in the retail portion of the shop. *07:30 – 22:30, daily* (**www.lusinespace.com**) 151/1 Dong Khoi (District 1) (+84 8 6674 9565) First Floor. Also a second location at 70 Le Loi (District 1) (+84 8 3521 0703)

Cafe Nguoi Saigon (#1) – This is an intimate, refined cafe off a side city corridor with a handful of tables. There is live, sultry music on Thursday nights by candle light. *11:00 – 22:00, daily* 71/4 Mac Thi Buoi (District 1)

ID Cafe (#5) – This is a cozy, old-school coffee shop hidden away up stairs, classically decorated with a comfortable amount of room to relax. It is a great spot to enjoy an excellent afternoon *ca phe sua da* (ice coffee). *07:00 – 22:30, daily* (**www.idcafe.net**) 34D Thu Khoa Huan (District 1) (+84 8 3822 2901)

Ru'nam Cafe (#2) – With perhaps the best cappuccino in town, you haven't tried one in Vietnam unless you try it at classy Ru'nam Cafe with freshly ground Vietnamese espresso beans. There are multiple, beautifully adorned floors in this glimpse of Vietnamese high society. There is a selection of delectable desserts available behind the counter glass to accompany your beverage, and a menu of light snacks. *07:00 – 23:00, daily* (**www.caferunam.com**) 96 Mac Thi Buoi (District 1) (+84 8 3825 8883)

Napoly Cafe – Well-dressed clientele gather at this Italian-style coffee shop that also serves breakfast and lunch, including many Italian specialties. Upstairs there is a snazzy bar open in the evenings often with live music. *18:00 – 01:00, daily* (**www.napolycafe.com**) 7 Pham Ngoc Thach (District 3)

Cuc Gach Cafe – This stylish, modern cafe with its retro record player is one of the architectural highlights of Ho Chi Minh City. There are traditional Vietnamese and other Asian dishes available, as well as outside seating. *07:00 – 22:30, daily* (**www.cucgachcafe.com**) 79 Phon Ke Binh (District 1)

Khanhcasa Tea House (#6, #11) – This is a cozy tea house with elegant snacks, a coffee shop, and a delectable dessert cafe all-in-one, with multiple thoughtfully-decorated floors and a well-positioned terrace with a view of the street action below. *07:00 – 22:30, daily* **(khanhcasateahouse.com)**
77 Ham Nghi Street (District 1) (+84 8 3825 7216)
48 Dong Khoi Street (District 1) (+84 8 3825 1756)

Cafe Suoi Da – Meaning "rocky stream," this outdoor cafe has a largely local clientele with outside seating among the garden to go along with some additional inside seating. Vietnamese dishes are available. *06:30 – 11:00, daily* 175 Nam Ky Khoi Nghia (District 3)

Highlands Coffee (#4) – This is a Vietnamese coffee chain founded in Hanoi, notable for pleasing local desserts, and with locations all over the city (also expanding internationally). There is a location directly behind the Opera House, and seventeen others in District 1 alone. *Most open early until 22:00 or 23:00, daily* **(www.highlandscoffee.com.vn)**

Phuc Long – Beginning in the 1950s as a provider of tea and tea products, it is now also a local cafe chain catering mostly to younger Vietnamese. Coffee, tea, fruit juices, and flavorful smoothies are available, with over a dozen cafes throughout the city. There is one at the corner of Phan Boi Chau Street and Le Loi Street near Ben Thanh Market. *Most open early until 22:00 or 23:00, daily* **(phuclong.com.vn)**

Starbucks – A recent phenomenon heralded by some and vilified as an incursion of Western commercialism by others, there are now several locations from this Seattle-based chain throughout the city. There are plans for many more, not just in Ho Chi Minh City, but throughout Vietnam. The original is two stories tall at 76 Le Lai Street (District 1) (+84 8 3823 9991) in a large space with a solid roster of desserts. The lines were quite long when they opened in 2013. Now it opens at 6:30 a.m. daily if you long for your early *café latte* while in Ho Chi Minh City. *Most open early until 23:00, daily*

Coffee Bean and Tea Leaf (#3) – Another international chain (based in Los Angeles, California and in twenty-five countries) with a few locations across the city. There is one across from Notre Dame Cathedral that makes an ideal perch for city-life watching. *Most open early until at least 21:00, daily* 235 Dong Khoi (District 1) (+84 8 3508 7285)

Where to Sleep

"Every dog is a lion at home." – Vietnamese Proverb

Ho Chi Minh City boasts a wide range of accommodations for all types of travelers and their lodging interests, from the beautiful French colonial classic hotels to the best of the international brands, and also great deals for the budget-conscious. These are all at a wide range of seasonally varying prices.

For the tourist, District 1 represents by far the best and most convenient location to stay in the entire city. The swanky, classic hotels tend be in the central area location of District 1 either on or not far from prominent, venerable Dong Khoi Street. In addition, most of the sights, restaurants, coffee shops, night clubs, and other listings in this book are in or near District 1.

The streets around Ben Thanh Market also are home to several smaller boutique hotels with substantial Vietnamese character. These choices are only a few blocks away from the primary downtown central district. The Pham Ngu Lao backpacker district provides some of the more budget-friendly options and also a couple of luxury options.

This book breaks the city's hotel offerings into five categories to help a traveler better choose an ideal, befitting location. The first is the "classic" category, with famous hotels, colonial charm, and other historical properties. These hotels are for those desiring a glimpse of the exotic past in the sophisticated, fanciful settings of the present. They come complete with top-notch service, wonderful restaurants, and welcoming, traditional Vietnamese charm. These are the properties where ghosts of the city's past are much more likely to be reflected in the hallway mirrors, and probably the best set of choices for the full Ho Chi Minh City experience.

The next category is the "Western and international brands" category, which can be more comfortable for the less adventurous, perhaps first-time visitors to the city. These choices are for those looking for familiar comforts and the quality service that the better chain hotels can provide. These hotels are well-known, often with more Western menus in the restaurants, and the employees will have a satisfactory command of English.

Then, there is the mid-range "other Asian and local hotels" category. These are stylish hotels with their own brand of charm, but perhaps not having quite the cachet as some of the more venerated local hotels. You will find some of the same welcoming, polite service as the classics with some tremendous dining offerings to match, but with a bit of a lighter price tag and not quite the same postcard experience.

Also, there are "serviced apartments" available which are more ideal for longer-term stays and family visits. They include amenities such as washers, dryers, and kitchenettes and generally provide more space, including separate bedrooms.

Finally, there are the "mini-hotels." These are locally owned, locally run, well-kept hotels that serve fine breakfasts, ordinarily have anywhere from fifteen to thirty rooms available, possess all the standard hotel comforts, and provide tremendous value vis-à-vis the other hotels. These are all highly recommended when you consider the value-for-price ratio. Experienced Ho Chi Minh City travelers find themselves gravitating to these mini-hotels, not only for the value, but for a more authentic, local Vietnamese experience.

Hotels in every category can be booked online, but most also allow walk-up reservations if you are in a pinch. Of course, you can also book via telephone.

If you book in advance, reconfirm within a few days of your stay because of the difficulty language barriers can trigger, and because of international flights showing up at any hour of the night. You don't want to arrive at 2 a.m. after traveling twenty hours to find your name not written in the hotel book, or that someone with a similar name canceled your reservation by mistake, and that there are no more rooms available. The phone call or email is worth the effort.

If you pay for a room in cash at check-in, be sure to obtain a hotel-labeled receipt for cash paid to avoid any misunderstandings and difficulties at check-out.

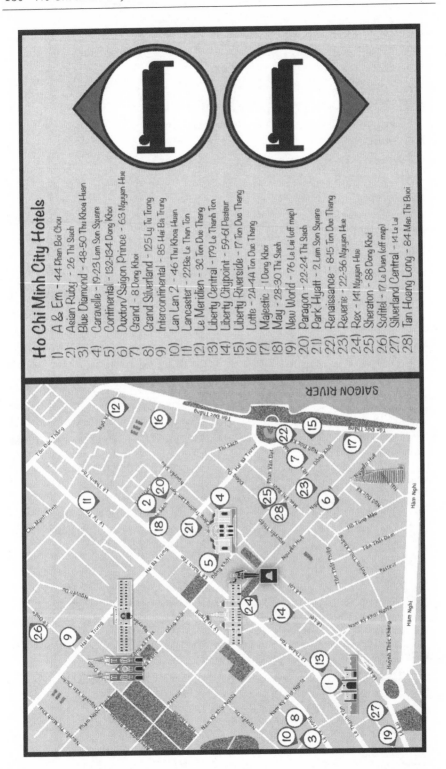

Ho Chi Minh City Hotels

1) A & Em – 44 Phan Boi Chau
2) Asian Ruby – 26 Thi Sach
3) Blue Diamond – 48-50 Thu Khoa Huan
4) Caravelle – 19-23 Lam Son Square
5) Continental – 132-134 Dong Khoi
6) Duxton/Saigon Prince – 63 Nguyen Hue
7) Grand – 8 Dong Khoi
8) Grand Silverland – 125 Ly Tu Trong
9) Intercontinental – 85 Hai Ba Trung
10) Lan Lan 2 – 46 Thu Khoa Huan
11) Lancaster – 22Bis Le Thanh Ton
12) Le Meridien – 30 Ton Duc Thang
13) Liberty Central – 179 Le Thanh Ton
14) Liberty Citypoint – 59-61 Pasteur
15) Liberty Riverside – 17 Ton Duc Thang
16) Lotte – 2A-4A Ton Duc Thang
17) Majestic – 1 Dong Khoi
18) May – 28-30 Thi Sach
19) New World – 76 La Lai (off map)
20) Paragon – 22-24 Thi Sach
21) Park Hyatt – 2 Lam Son Square
22) Renaissance – 8-15 Ton Duc Thang
23) Reverie – 22-36 Nguyen Hue
24) Rex – 141 Nguyen Hue
25) Sheraton – 88 Dong Khoi
26) Sofitel – 17 Le Duan (off map)
27) Silverland Central – 14 La Lai
28) Tan Hoang Long – 84 Mac Thi Buoi

Price Key (USD):

$ - Up to $50/night
$$ - $50-$100/night
$$$ - $100-$150/night
$$$$ - $150+/night

Classic Hotels

$$ **Majestic Hotel** (#17, Central) – The Majestic Hotel was opened in 1925 and is adjacent to and overlooks the Saigon River. This grand location was occupied and used as barracks by Japanese Imperial Forces during the Second World War. Its rooftop bar was a favorite of Graham Greene and his fictional Thomas Fowler character in his novel *The Quiet American*, mostly because of the views of the Saigon River and the cool evening breezes the river provides. Other luminaries to stay here include Somerset Maugham, French actress Catherine Deneuve, Britain's Prince Andrew, and multiple foreign presidents and prime ministers. It is well known that French colonial agents often met with spies at this hotel, and that it was a point of spy rendezvous during the Vietnam War. Grenade grills covered the windows of the Vietnamese Cyclo Restaurant within the hotel during the Vietnam War to protect diners from shrapnel. These days, it is a mostly quiet, charming hotel in a first-rate location. It boasts 175 rooms, six restaurants, and some of the more classic Golden Age architecture in all of Ho Chi Minh City. (**www.majesticsaigon.com**) 1 Dong Khoi (District 1) (+84 8 3829 5517)

$$ **Hotel Continental** (#5, Central) – The Hotel Continental was opened in 1880 and was the first palatial hotel in the city. For a long time after, it remained the grandest hotel in all of Saigon. Located in the heart of the city on Dong Khoi Street across from the opera house, it is now a property of the state-owned Saigon Tourist. Perhaps it is not quite as grand as it was in its heyday during the French colonial era, but it still maintains its original colonial architecture and is beautifully appointed. It maintains its historical all-white exterior

paint, the color originally chosen to prevent the absorption of the city's famous scorching heat from the sun. Many scenes from Graham Greene's *The Quiet American* novel took place here at the hotel and on its terrace. Since its beginning, the hotel has been frequented by upscale business folk, journalists, well-to-do tourists and politically connected crowds. During the Vietnam War, it served as host to *Time* and *Newsweek* as both had their news bureaus here. It has a notable former guest list, including former French president Jacques Chirac. In addition to its eighty rooms, there is a classy French restaurant *Le Bourgeois*, a breakfast buffet, and a streetside cafe, a pleasant city-watching spot for an afternoon ice coffee. There is also an elegant inner courtyard adorned with frangipani trees, and the notable Starrynite Bar with its award-winning bartenders. The hotel is in a great location and of great appeal to those with an interest in Ho Chi Minh City's colonial past. (**www.continentalsaigon.com**) 132-134 Dong Khoi (District 1) (+84 8 3829 0936)

$$$ **Caravelle Saigon** (#4, Central) – The Caravelle Hotel has a significant wartime legacy. It was opened in 1959 and is state-owned by Saigon Tourist. Its location in the heart of Ho Chi Minh City makes it an ideal spot for tourists with all the major sights in walking distance. Its famous Saigon Saigon Bar on the ninth floor of the older hotel of its two hotel structures (a newer twenty-four-story addition was added) was a famous watering hole for foreign journalists during the Vietnam War. Correspondents would watch the war unfold on the outskirts of the city because of the top-floor view, which now provides a great view of Dong Khoi Street and the rest of the city. The hotel is famous for a bomb that exploded here in 1964 targeting foreign journalists (fortunately there were no fatalities to accompany the explosion). It was also the location presumably of several meetings held in secret that were critical of South Vietnam President Ngo Dinh Diem prior to the coup that removed him. It was the home of Australian and New Zealand embassies, and the headquarters of NBC, ABC, and CBS during the Vietnam War. The Saigon Saigon Bar still is lively these days, with live music and a solid list of cocktails in the evening. There is a champagne bar, a martini bar, and the "Club Las Vegas" casino in the hotel. For meals, "Reflections" fine dining and "19 Buffet" are available to keep you from going hungry. You can

catch live lounge singing and music in the lobby most nights to enjoy while having a drink. (**www.caravellehotel.com**) 19-23 Lam Son Square (District 1) (+84 8 3823 4999)

$$$ **Rex Hotel** (#24, Central) – The 286-room Rex Hotel is the hotel most associated with wartime Vietnam. Built as an auto showroom in 1927 and opened as a hotel in 1961, it is now owned by Saigon Tourist. The rooftop bar was a place where officers and journalists hung out during the Vietnam War, often watching flashes and hearing explosions in the distance. It was the location of the daily news conference from the American military command known as the Five O'clock Follies, so named based on suspicions that complete information was not being provided to journalists from military leaders, and that some of it was perhaps misleading. The hotel is in the heart of downtown Ho Chi Minh City. It has two outdoor swimming pools that overlook the city, a rooftop tennis court, a spa, and numerous high-end fashion shops such as Cartier and Rolex. The hotel has a total of six restaurants, with Vietnamese and other Asian fare available. The Hoa Mai restaurant occasionally has traditional dancing shows. There is also a casino. Even if you are not staying here, it is a fun location for a few early-evening rooftop cocktails to take the whole of the city in. (**www.rexhotelvietnam.com**) 141 Nguyen Hue (District 1) (+84 8 3829 2185)

Western and International Brands

$$$$ **Park Hyatt** (#21, Central) – Beautiful, refined, prestigious, and grand, the Park Hyatt was built in a modern interpretation of French colonial style. It was closed for a major renovation much of 2015. It is one of the top hotels in the city and is in a prominent location with 245 luxurious rooms and suites. It offers an Italian restaurant, an Asian and Western restaurant (see Square One in *Where to Eat*), and a night establishment. There is a splendid coffee and tea lounge to opulently and comfortably escape the afternoon heat, recommended even if you are not staying here. With professional, sophisticated

service throughout the hotel, there is also a spectacular pool and a wonderfully relaxing spa. The building is on the site of the old Brinks Hotel, which housed American officers and was bombed during the Vietnam War in 1964, killing two Americans (today a memorial stands on the lawn at the corner of Lam Son Square and Hai Ba Trung Street). (**saigon.park.hyatt.com**) 2 Lam Son Square (District 1) (+84 8 3824 1234)

$$$ **Sheraton** (#25, Central) – Before the Park Hyatt and Reverie arrived to challenge, the Sheraton was the top luxury option in town. With 485 rooms and suites (including 118 in the newer Grand Tower), the Sheraton is located in the heart of Ho Chi Minh City on Dong Khoi Street near Lam Son Square. Along with its grand lobby, it is known for its rooftop bar (with views from its outdoor terrace), nightclub, and signature Pan-Asian restaurant on the 23rd floor. There is a Cantonese Dim Sum restaurant, multiple cafes, a lounge, a sprawling international buffet, and 24-hour in-room dining available. The pool, spa, business center, and over 2500 square feet of meeting space round out the hotel. (**www.sheratonsaigon.com**) 88 Dong Khoi (District 1) (+84 8 3827 2828)

$$$ **Le Meridien** (#12, Central) – Newly opened in 2015, the 350-room, twenty-six-suite Le Meridian is perched next to the Saigon River. It is in walking distance to Dong Khoi Street and downtown Ho Chi Minh City. It is close to several of the restaurants and the varied nightlife on Le Thanh Ton Street as well. European-style modernity, chic design, and a bright color scheme highlight the experience, as does the infinity pool and a well-equipped fitness room on the ninth floor with views overlooking the river. There are multiple restaurants, including the Last Recipe restaurant that has an indulgent breakfast buffet available offering Vietnamese, Chinese, Japanese, and Western cuisine with a view of the river. There is also an Asian restaurant, a pastry bar, a serene, relaxing cafe area with coffee drinks and an oeno wine machine for wine tasting. There is also a poolside bar, and Bamboo Chic, an Asian bar and restaurant. (**www.starwoodhotels.com/lemeridien/property/overview/index.html?propertyID=3529**) 3C Ton Duc Thang (District 1) (+84 8 6263 6688)

$$$ **Sofitel Saigon Plaza** (#26, Central) – This hotel, a block from Hai Ba Trung Street and two blocks from Notre Dame, is in a quieter location of District 1 across from the old South Vietnam United States Embassy complex (now the US Consulate). It has 286 modern rooms, including eleven suites. Highlights include a twenty-five-meter rooftop pool with spectacular city views, the sultry and classy Boudoir Lounge wine and cocktail bar, Mezz restaurant, an international buffet with a wonderful spread of Vietnamese, Pan-Asian, and international fare, and a tiny gourmet shop. The French restaurant L'Olivier frequently hosts various visiting Michelin-starred chefs for months at a time. There is a business center with multiple computers and offices, and a sizable fitness center with free weights and a spa. The hotel is a couple of blocks walk to get to downtown. (**www.accorhotels.com/gb/hotel-2077-sofitel-saigon-plaza/index.shtml**) 17 Le Duan (District 1) (+84 8 3824 1555)

$$$ **Novotel Saigon Centre** (Central) – A few blocks away from the action on the edges of District 1 and District 3, the newly built, pleasant Novotel Hotel boasts 247 rooms with an open-air "indoor" pool, and multiple international restaurants. There is a snazzy outdoor rooftop bar with great views, a tempting selection of "Vietnamese tapas," and likely the best cheese selection in town. (**www.accorhotels.com/gb/hotel-7965-novotel-saigon-centre/index.shtml**) 167 Hai Ba Trung (District 3) (+84 8 3822 4866)

$$$ **Intercontinental Asiana Saigon** (#9, Central) – The modern-Italian architecture (built in 2009) of the Intercontinental is walkable to downtown Ho Chi Minh City and other major sights in town. It is part of the Kumho Asiana (a Korean tire company) Plaza, which has several international restaurants, including the Hard Rock Cafe music venue (see *Nightlife*). It has 305 large rooms and suites, several dining options, and lots of nearby entertainment. Longer-term serviced apartment stays are available via Intercontinental Residences (see the website for more information). While an official address number is not given by the hotel, it is approximately at 85 Hai Ba Trung Street for GPS purposes. (**www.ihg.com**) Le Duan & Hai Ba Trung (District 1) (+84-8 3520 9999)

$$$ **Renaissance Riverside** (#22, Central) – Overlooking the Saigon River, the Marriott-owned Renaissance Riverside has 336 rooms and suites, a large lobby, central atrium, and top-notch service. It is in an attractive location a block from where Dong Khoi Street meets the river. There is a spa, rooftop pool, and a gym. There are multiple dining options including a Chinese restaurant, an all-day international buffet, and several cafes. (**www.marriott.com**) 8-15 Ton Duc Thang (District 1) (+84 8 3822 0033)

$$$ **Pullman Saigon Centre** (Pham Ngu Lao) – The Pullman Saigon Centre offers over three hundred stylish rooms in proximity to Bui Vien and the backpacker district of Ho Chi Minh City. The Pullman upscale business-traveler chain is now part of the French-based Accor Hotels Group (along with Sofitel and several others). Cobalt, a tapas restaurant on the thirtieth floor with a trendy wine bar, also has a rooftop sky bar–great for a cocktail to take in the night-time views. There is also a well-supplied buffet restaurant available for breakfast through dinner. (**www.pullmanhotels.com**) 148 Tran Hung Dao (District 1) (+84 8 3838 8686)

Other Asian and Local Hotels

$$$$ **The Reverie** (#23, Central) – The Reverie Hotel Saigon, opened in 2015, is perhaps the swankiest, highest-priced option in Ho Chi Minh City. This world-class, Italian-designed hotel occupies the top floors of the thirty-nine-story downtown Times Square building. It will wow you with its lavish glass, marble, and classical artistic decor (where both Asian and Italian architectural elements have been successfully blended). It boasts a city-block-long bar (it's actually nearly fifty yards long) and great views over the city and Saigon River. Mercedes and Rolls Royce transportation for use around town is available for guests, and there is even underwater music in the outdoor deck swimming pool high above the city. The Royal Pavilion is a beautiful Cantonese restaurant. There are many high-end shops on the

lower floors. There is also the beautiful, classy R&J Italian restaurant (as in Romeo & Juliet) with a *degustazione* menu to match the theme of the hotel. (**www.thereveriesaigon.com**) 22-36 Nguyen Hue (District 1) (+84 8 3823 6688)

$$ **Grand Hotel** (#7, Central) – Built in 1930 near the river on Dong Khoi Street in the heart of the city, the historic Grand Hotel provides 230 vintage rooms and suites. With chandeliered, classical elegance, it boasts the Saigon Palace Restaurant on the second floor. It is also well known for its nightly rooftop piano music bar on the twentieth floor of the new wing (built in 2011) that provides views of the river and downtown. (**www.grandhotel.vn**) 8 Dong Khoi (District 1) (+84 8 3824 5778)

$$$ **New World Saigon** (#19, Ben Thanh) – Hong Kong-based New World Hotels and Resorts' Saigon hotel is the top luxury hotel in the Ben Thanh Market area. With 533 rooms, a rooftop swimming pool that serves as an oasis to the madness of the city (along with a nifty poolside bar), three restaurants serving Asian, Japanese, and international cuisine, a spa, a fitness center, and a coffee shop with light jazz, the New World is an attractive, centrally located base to hang your hat while in Ho Chi Minh City. President Bill Clinton and First Lady Hillary thought so in 2000. (**saigon.newworldhotels.com**) 76 Le Lai (District 1) (+84 8 3822 8888)

$$ **Saigon Prince** (#6, formerly the Duxton Hotel, Central) – The newly remodeled Saigon Prince, Singaporean-owned, is a sophisticated, spacious hotel in a premier downtown location on Nguyen Hue Boulevard. There are 181 rooms, six club suites, and four apartments that span two levels. It has a restaurant, lounge, outdoor pool, gym, and spa. (**www.saigonprincehotel.com**) 63 Nguyen Hue (District 1) (+84 8 3822 2999)

$$$ **Lotte** (#16, Central) – On the Saigon River and a few blocks walk from downtown, this South Korea-based hotel has 283 rooms, a large resort-like pool, waterfall, often a pianist in the grand, high-ceiling lobby, and business facilities. Comfortable, quiet rooms are accentuated by a professional staff. Restaurants include an

international buffet, a Cantonese restaurant, a Japanese restaurant, and a steakhouse/bar. (**www.lottehotel.com/saigon/en**) 2A-4A Ton Duc Thang (District 1) (+84 8 3823 3333)

$$$ **Liberty Central Saigon Citypoint** (#14, Central) – A new addition to the city's hotel landscape in 2014, this hotel boasts a great location on the corner of Pasteur and Le Loi approximately halfway between Ben Thanh Market and Dong Khoi Street. It boasts spacious modern rooms, the Central Restaurant with both international dishes and Vietnamese dishes (including a breakfast buffet), a bistro and coffee lounge with live music nightly, a six-theater cinema, a spa, and a rooftop pool and sky bar that gives the hotel an innovatively chic feel. Contemporary rooms offer views of downtown. (**www.odysseahotels.com/saigon-city-point-hotel**) 59-61 Pasteur (District 1) (+84 8 3822 5678)

$$$ **Liberty Central Saigon Centre** (#13, Ben Thanh) – Closer to Ben Thanh Market than its newer counterpart (yet still close to downtown), this hotel's 140 comfortable rooms come with a rooftop pool that has great views (especially in the evening), a spa and health club, the Central restaurant, and a bistro. (**www.odysseahotels.com/saigon-centre-hotel**) 179 Le Thanh Ton (District 1) (+84 8 3823 9269)

$$$ **Liberty Riverside** (#15, Central) – Situated on the Saigon River, the Liberty Riverside hotel is third hotel of the Liberty Hotels trilogy. Its 170 contemporary rooms have either river or city views. There are multiple restaurants serving international and Vietnamese fare, a rooftop pool, a sky bar, spa, and health center. (**www.odysseahotels.com/riverside-hotel**) 17 Ton Duc Thang (District 1) (+84 8 3827 1717)

$$$ **Villa Song** (District 2) – Perched in a majestic, palatial, colonial villa upstream from downtown on the Saigon River in District 2, the Villa Song is an elegant, calm retreat away from the cacophony of the heart of Ho Chi Minh City. Each of its newly renovated twenty-three rooms and suites is individually designed, and the hotel is also enhanced with its grand river terrace. There is an outdoor pool, spa,

and a riverside restaurant that features candlelit dining at night. There is an outdoor cocktail bar for sumptuous tropical drinks. There are several shuttle boat rides available each day that take you down river to a pier that's a five-minute walk from downtown Ho Chi Minh City. (**www.villasong.com**) 197/2 Nguyen Van Huong (District 2) (+84 8 3744 6090)

Serviced Apartments

$$ **The Lancaster** (#11, Central) – This serviced apartment offers 109 units, including studios, one-, two-, and three-bedroom options, and penthouse units in the heart of "Japan Town." There is laundry available, daily cleaning service, and kitchenettes. Although there is no on-site restaurant, the dressy Sin Lounge cocktail bar offers drinks and some evening entertainment. The Lancaster is on Le Than Ton, a street dotted with several restaurants and multifarious nightlife. (**www.lancaster.com.vn**) 22Bis Le Than Ton (District 1) (+84 8 3824 6666)

$$ **Sherwood Residence** (Central) – A bit of a walk to downtown, the Sherwood offers 228 two-bedroom, three-bedroom, and penthouse units. It has a private restaurant, swimming pool, fitness center, library, and mini-theater. (**www.sherwoodresidence.com**) 127 Pasteur (District 3) (84 8 3823 2288)

Mini and Boutique Hotels

$$ **A&Em Ben Thanh** (#1, Ben Thanh) – There are several A&Em mini-hotels around town, all having attractive rates and of sound value. A favorite is on Phan Boi Chou Street, adjacent to Ben Thanh Market. At that location, there is a comfortable, outdoor sitting area next to the market action (including the night market), an ideal perch for relaxing and cooling off with a refreshing drink in the afternoon or

early evening. The slightly more expensive VIP rooms have a seventies-era feel to them. There is a sizable lobby and a well-executed Vietnamese breakfast buffet served each morning. The staff is friendly and helpful. (**www.a-emhotels.com**) 44 Phan Boi Chou (District 1) (+84 8 3915 2727)

$$ **Paragon** (#20, Central) – With a large lobby and lounge area, the Paragon offers a spa and restaurant in addition to its sleeping quarters. Rooms are a little meager, but proximity to Hai Ba Trung Street is a plus. (**www.paragonsaigon.com**) 22-24 Thi Sach (District 1) (+84 8 3823 3999)

$$ **May** (#18, Central) – Another hotel on Thi Sach Street with 113 rooms, a buffet restaurant, fitness center, a larger than average swimming pool, and a spa. (**www.mayhotel.com.vn**) 28-30 Thi Sach (District 1) (+84 8 3823 4501)

$ **Asian Ruby** (#2, Central) – Frequently offering great deals, this hotel is wedged between the Paragon and the May Hotel. It has an ornately decorated lobby and eighty recently remodeled rooms with wooden floors. With its restaurant and bar, it is another pleasant economical option on Thi Sach Street. (**www.asianrubyhotel.com**) 26 Thi Sach (District 1) (+84 8 3827 2838)

$$ **Blue Diamond** (#3, Ben Thanh) – This mini-hotel is located near Ben Thanh Market with comfortable, classic rooms and a restaurant serving Vietnamese and Western fare. (**www.bluediamondhotel.com.vn**) 48-50 Thu Khoa Huan (District 1) (+84 8 3823 6167)

$ **Silverland Central** (#27, Ben Thanh) – There are several Silverland hotels around town, and the Silverland Central is a solid choice conveniently located next to Ben Thanh Market. It has a trendy hot spot bar on the roof (serving international cuisine) with great views over the market, an additional restaurant, a coffee bar, and a lounge. (**www.silverlandhotels.com/silver-land-central-hotel-spa.html**) 14 Le Lai (District 1) (+84 8 3827 2738)

$$ Grand Silverland (#8, Ben Thanh) – The newest of the Silverland collection is also near Ben Thanh Market with a great rooftop bar and pool. Its eighty-nine rooms and suites, roof garden restaurant, and relaxing spa make it a smart choice. (**www.silverlandhotels.com/grand-silverland-hotel-spa.html**) 125 Ly Tu Trong (District 1) (+84 8 3829 3888)

$ Lan Lan 2 (#10, Ben Thanh) – With over one hundred cozy rooms and situated a block from Ben Thanh Market, the Lan Lan 2 and its Asian breakfast buffet is an excellent budget choice. (**lanlanhotel.com.vn**) 46 Thu Khoa Huan (District 1) (+84 8 3822 7926)

$ Tan Hoang Long (#28, Central) – This is a convenient hotel with spacious rooms in a great location near the center of town. It is on Mac Thi Buoi Street on the block that connects Nguyen Hue Boulevard and Dong Khoi Street. Lots of restaurants, cafes, and entertainment abound on this city block and it serves as a great base for walking the city. (**www.tanhoanglong-hotel.com**) 84 Mac Thi Buoi (District 1) (+84 8 3827 0006)

$ Bich Duyen (Pham Ngu Lao) – Cheap, charming little hotel down a side street in the heart of the backpacker district. (**bichduyenhotel.net**) 283/4 Pham Ngu Lao (District 1) (+84 8 3837 4588)

$ Cinnamon Hotel (Pham Ngu Lao) – Comfortable, well-maintained hotel with spacious rooms. (**www.cinnamonhotel.net**) 74 Le Thi Rieng (District 1) (+84 8 3926 0130)

Nightlife

"If you go out a lot at night, you will probably meet ghosts." –
Vietnamese Proverb

From rooftop clubs with tremendous views to rocking classic music venues, Ho Chi Minh City's electric nightlife scene has something for everybody. The revelry at nightfall can be raucous and loud at times, but it can also be a great source of good old-fashioned fun. There is a plethora of musical talent around, and many places to imbibe local cocktails. While many bars and clubs close by midnight and only a handful stay open late, the evening comes alive in the city when the daytime heat starts to fade.

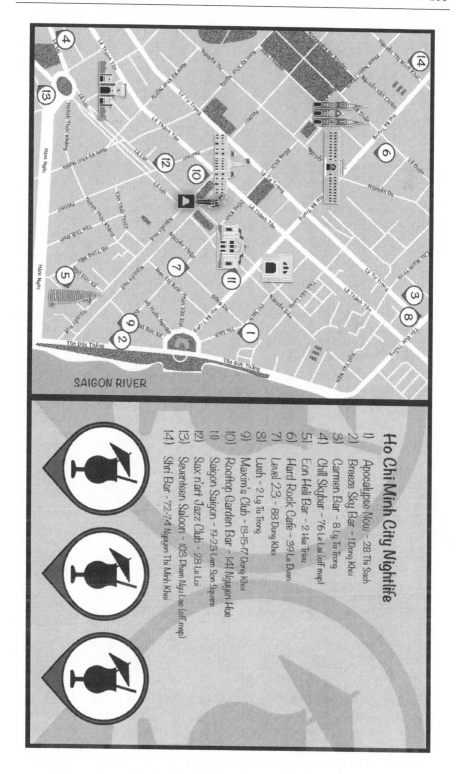

Ho Chi Minh City Nightlife

1) Apocalypse Now - 2B Thi Sach
2) Breeze Sky Bar - 1 Dong Khoi
3) Carmen Bar - 8 Ly Tu Trong
4) Chill Skybar - 76 Le Lai (off map)
5) Eon Heli Bar - 2 Hai Trieu
6) Hard Rock Cafe - 39 Le Duan
7) Level 23 - 88 Dong Khoi
8) Lush - 2 Ly Tu Trong
9) Maxim's Club - 13-15-17 Dong Khoi
10) Rooftop Garden Bar - 141 Nguyen Hue
11) Saigon Saigon - 19-23 Lam Son Square
12) Sax n'art Jazz Club - 28 Le Loi
13) Seventeen Saloon - 103 Pham Ngu Lao (off map)
14) Shri Bar - 72-74 Nguyen Thi Minh Khai

Rooftop Bars

With the warm weather that begins to cool off a little at twilight, rooftop bars and their clear evening views are magnificent in Ho Chi Minh City. Here are some of the best:

Chill Skybar (#4, AB Tower) – This ultra-chic, modern rooftop bar not far from Ben Thanh Market is the happening place to be for locals, tourists, and ex-pats to strut their stuff in the sky. Patrons primarily present themselves wearing dapper yet playful outfits with fancy, creative cocktails in hand. There is a spectacular, round, color-shifting outdoor bar with several fast-moving bartenders, providing a stunning view of the Ho Chi Minh City skyline from on high. Some of the more beautiful people in town can be found dancing, socializing, and engaging in fits of revelry in the evening air in a Las Vegas-like upscale atmosphere (drinks are cheaper at happy hour if you are on a budget). Reservations recommended for a table. *17:30 – late, daily* (**www.chillsaigon.com**) 76 Le Lai (District 1) (+84 8 6253 8888)

Level 23 Nightspot & Wine Bar (#7, Sheraton Hotel) – Level 23 Nightspot is a "be seen" club with live music and dancing on top of the Sheraton Hotel on Dong Khoi Street. The outside wine bar has a broad, open, bird's eye view of the city below encompassing a 180-degree after-hours aspect of the city's blend of old and new architecture. It is usually a tranquil spot for a more relaxing evening in a pleasant atmosphere. *18:00 – 01:00, daily (wine bar opens 12:00)* (**www.level23saigon.com**) 88 Dong Khoi (District 1) (+84 8 3827 2828)

Pandora (HDTC Tower) – With a selectively chosen wine and cocktail list, clear evening views, well-dressed younger clientele, and intimate candlelit tables, Pandora is a favorite among younger local business professionals. While not cheap, it is one of the classier places in town. It will require public transportation from downtown locations. *18:00 – 03:00, daily* (**www.facebook.com/PandoraSkyLounge**) HDTC Tower, 36 Bui Thi Xuan (District 1) (+84 8 3926 0455)

Breeze Sky Bar (#2, Majestic Hotel) – Famous as a nightly watering hole for journalist Thomas Fowler in Graham Greene's *The Quiet American* novel and subsequent film adaptations, this rooftop bar has some remaining colonial period ambiance. It is on the roof of the Majestic Hotel at the end of Dong Khoi Street and has views of the Saigon River and the emerging District 2 on the other side of the river. There is live music some nights, but it is for the most part a quiet location. *10:30 – 24:00, daily* (**www.majesticsaigon.com**) 1 Dong Khoi (District 1) (+84 8 3829 5517)

Shri Bar (#14, Centec Building) – Shri is an attractive, contemporary cocktail lounge and terrace with panoramic rooftop views overlooking all of downtown from a few blocks away. It also has a European-style restaurant with terrace seating (see *Where to Eat* for more details). *10:30 – 24:00, daily* (**www.shri.vn**) 72-74 Nguyen Thi Minh Khai (District 3) (+84 8 3827 9631)

Saigon Saigon (#11, Caravelle Hotel) – This is a cocktail bar on top of the Caravelle Hotel with live music, "Top 40" covers and sometimes Latin tunes with other international variety. Come for the great views. It was a favorite sky den of journalists during the Vietnam War who tragically could watch explosions in the distance as the conflict unfolded. Live entertainment starts at 9 p.m. *11:00 – 24:00, daily* (**www.caravellehotel.com**) 19-23 Lam Son Square (District 1) (+84 8 3823 4999)

Rooftop Garden Bar (#10, Rex Hotel) – With a dramatic, quiet view over the heart of the city with enticing but expensive cocktails, this bar is famous for its ties to the Vietnam War. Members of the military and journalists would often wind down here. It was also the location of nightly press conferences during the war (see *Walking Tour* for more details). *06:00 – late, daily* (**www.rexhotelvietnam.com**) 141 Nguyen Hue (District 1) (+84 8 3829 2185)

Eon Heli Bar (#5, Bitexco Financial Tower) – While technically not a rooftop bar, it's the highest bar in the city with spectacular window views from the fifty-first floor of the Bitexco Financial Tower. There is live music most nights, and window seats available away from the loudness. There is a coffee shop on the floor above and a restaurant on the floor below, all with the same spectacular views. *10:30 – late, daily* (**www.eon51.com**) 2 Hai Trieu (District 1) (+84 8 6291 8751)

Air 360 Sky Lounge – For the younger crowd with open rooftop views and loud, head-quaking dance music. *17:30 – 01:00 (24:00 Sunday), daily* (**air360skylounge.com**) 136-138 Le Thi Hong Gam (District 1) (+84 8 7303 8888)

Live Music

Seventeen Saloon (#13) – Although there is a country and western coyote bar vibe to the decor to go along with its cowboy-hatted waitresses, the place is known for its nightly rock-n-roll shows. It is more akin to a local version of the House of Blues meets Hooters. While the cowgirls bring an endless stream of cold beer, sit back and enjoy American rock cover songs (from AC/DC to the Cranberries). Mostly, but not always, the music is provided by energetic and talented Filipino musicians, often with creative and entertaining performances. *19:00 – 04:00, daily* (**www.17saloon.vn**) 103 Pham Ngu Lao (District 1) (+84 8 3914 0007)

Acoustic Bar - Down an alley (look for the upside-down Volkswagen Bug) and often packed with music lovers, the Acoustic Bar features an array of local talented top acts, male and female, young and old, to thrill the attentive crowd. The audience consists mostly of young Vietnamese interspersed with a handful of in-the-know tourists, with covers and original music performed by multiple musicians. The chairs and couches allow you to be up close and intimate with the talented performers. *07:30 – 23:30, daily* (**www.facebook.com/acousticbarpage**) 6E Ngo Thoi Nhiem (District 3) (+84 127 677 7773)

Local musicians performing at the Acoustic Bar

Hard Rock Cafe (#6, Kumho Asiana Complex) – When you arrive, make sure you go to the basement where the live jamming is. The large, impressive venue, with a great sound system and stage lights to match, is a perfect place to experience Asian-style hard rock (playing mostly American cover songs), as bands from all over the continent cycle through. Similar to a Hard Rock Cafe anywhere, there is plenty of rock-n-roll memorabilia on display and several servers bringing armloads of cocktails, wine, and beer from the bar. You can also order American classics for dinner such as a burger and barbecue ribs if you desire a break from Vietnamese cuisine, or happened to have missed dinner. Your ears might be ringing on the way out. *11:00 – 24:00, daily* (**www.hardrock.com/cafes/ho-chi-minh-city**) 39 Le Duan (District 1) (+84 8 6291 7595)

Carmen Bar (#3) – As you enter through the hole in the rock wall, you will arrive into a well-decorated, sizeable yet cozy bar with an Andalusian feel. On the menu is a well-crafted set of snacks and a tempting drink list catering to a smart casual crowd. The talented house band plays soulful Latin music with American favorites intermingled. *18:30 – 01:00, daily* (**carmenbarsaigon.com.vn**) 8 Ly Tu Trong (District 1) (+84 8 3829 7699)

Sax n' Art Jazz Club (#12) – This is perhaps the top jazz club in Ho Chi Minh City. The house saxophonist and owner is Tran Manh Tuan (check out his YouTube clips). You will hear Vietnamese-influenced modern jazz, including favorites from John Coltrane and Charlie Parker every night after 9 p.m. on the nights Tuan is there. Near Ben Thanh Market on Le Loi Street, traveling jazz musicians are known to frequent the establishment. It is a great spot for jazz lovers but can be a little loud for old-timers. *19:00 – 24:00, daily* (**www.saxnart.com**) 28 Le Loi (District 1) (+84 8 8233 954)

Sixteen Club – In a scene from what feels like the seventies or an Austin Powers film in a posh basement below a restaurant, a talented house band plays Vietnamese music with several vocalists who cycle through on a given night. It's a favorite of returning Vietnamese expats. *19:00 – 24:00, daily*
16 Le Quy Don (District 3) (+84 8 934 7643)

Other Clubs

Apocalypse Now (#1) – A long time hot spot (open since 1991), this is one of Ho Chi Minh City's high-energy discotheques that rocks late into the night with a dance area, multiple bars, and an outdoor terrace. A mix of locals, expats, and tourists congregate here at night, all looking for a fun time. The action typically doesn't get going until after 11 p.m. or so. *19:00 – 04:00, daily*
(**www.apocalypsesaigon.com**) 2B Thi Sach (District 1) (+84 8 3825 6124)

Maxim's Club (#9, Majestic Hotel) – A classic "Old Saigon" live music ballroom dancing bar and club since 1925, the venerable Maxim's Club was reopened in 2012 with Vietnamese and international musicians providing the backdrop for the waltz and the rumba. An expensive cocktails and spirits menu caters to a dressy, classy, older clientele. *19:00 – 00:30, daily* (**www.maxims.com.vn**)
13-15-17 Dong Khoi (District 1) (+84 8 3822 5554)

Lush Saigon (#8) – Lush is a see-and-be-seen, in vogue, thumping dance club that is more than a decade old. It still has trend-setting interiors and stays lively well into the night. You will find a mix of young locals, tourists, and expats. There is also an outside back garden for socializing into the wee hours. *20:00 – 02:00, daily*
(**www.facebook.com/LushSaigon**) 2 Ly Tu Trong (District 1) (+84 8 3824 2496)

Tours and Activities

There is an intriguing, comprehensive and varied collection of tours and activities on offer in Ho Chi Minh City, including motorbike tours, cooking classes, guided walks, and art tours. Different activities are available in the morning, afternoon, and evening, so you can always find something to do at all parts of the day. These activities are also a great opportunity to meet some knowledgeable local folk for some native perspectives on a wide range of topics, and also a chance to interact with other tourists from all over the world to share experiences and tips. Here is a selective sample of what is available.

Bike tours:

In the past several years, the concept of touring the city on the back of a motorbike with a local driver has proliferated substantially, primarily because it is not only fun, but also provides a chance to meet some amiable, cheerful, and engaging locals. You can see much of the city in just a few hours. Here are some of the more popular ones:

XO Tours – An all-female guided motorbike tour started by an American named Tung born in Vietnam who escaped Saigon with his family at the age of three. Tung, still the owner, was a securities trader in the United States. After a year of philanthropic work in Vietnam, he decided to stay and start the tour company. Tours of sights and a foodie tour are available and cover large parts of the city, including visits to several different districts. (**www.xotours.vn**)

Back of the Bike Tours – Created by professional American chefs, their tour lineup includes a custom, deep-dive chef's tour. (**www.backofthebiketours.com**)

Vespa Adventures – Vespa offers several tours in Ho Chi Minh City, and also some long distance and multi-day tours including trips deep into the Mekong Delta region. (**www.vespaadventures.com**)

Tiger Tours – Provides several city tours throughout Ho Chi Minh City. (**www.mytigertour.com**)

Other Tours and Tour Groups:

Les Rives – This company provides luxury speedboat tours to hidden places where roads cannot take you, including a two-day Mekong River tour and a sunset cruise. (**lesrivesexperience.com**)

Hoa Tuc Vietnamese Cooking Class – This is a great hands-on cooking class with experienced Vietnamese chefs, consisting of up to twelve people per half-day class, with each student cooking their own dishes as part of the instruction. Class starts with a trip to Ben Thanh Market to procure fresh ingredients. The course provides a different menu every day for those who want to return multiple times. This is a great introduction to the core tenets of the local version of Vietnamese cuisine. (**www.saigoncookingclass.com**)

Trails and Tales – Trails and Tales offers a historical walking tour of Ho Chi Minh City. On Saturdays only, it's given by Adam, a local teacher from England who now lives in Ho Chi Minh City with his Vietnamese wife. (**www.trailstalessaigon.com**)

Sophie's Art Tour – To gain an appreciation of artistic Ho Chi Minh City, check out Sophie's Art Tour. The tour visits private collections, museums, and contemporary art spaces in a four-hour tour that is given five days per week. (**www.sophiesarttour.com**)

Exo Travel – Formerly called Exotissimo, this tour company is professionally run with complete travel packages in Vietnam and throughout Southeast Asia, including day trips down the Mekong River. (**www.exotravel.com**)

Urban Adventures – Operating tours around the world, Urban's offerings in Ho Chi Minh City include city tours, the Mekong Delta, and a nighttime street food tour.
(**www.urbanadventures.com/destination/ho-chi-minh-city-tours**)

Shopping

Most of the souvenirs you will buy in Ho Chi Minh City will likely be purchased in Ben Thanh Market, on and around Le Loi Street, or on Dong Khoi Street. You can negotiate favorable deals in these places. To do better in price, visit Cholon in District 5, including markets such as Binh Tay. Cholon is where many of the vendors in District 1 purchase their goods, and then mark them up for sale to tourists. It is essentially a wholesale market. It is fifteen to twenty minutes by taxi or Uber from Ben Thanh Market. An Dong Market in District 10 is an alternative to Ben Thanh Market as well.

Classic souvenirs and gifts include chopsticks, local coffee, tea sets, handicrafts, art, jewelry, bowls, dishes, traditional *ao dai* dresses, other apparel (including tailor-made), accessories, junk-boat replicas, artist tools, local candy, and dried food.

For high-end retail shopping, there is Diamond Plaza, Parkson, Vincom Center, Union Square, and the shops in around the luxury hotels of District 1, such as the Rex Hotel and the Reverie.

Nguyen Trai Street, starting in District 1 a few blocks from Ben Thanh Market and leading into District 5, has a plentiful amount of clothing, footwear, and many other miscellaneous shops, along with several casual eateries. It can be a great place to spend an afternoon devoted to browsing from store to store.

Specialty Shops

In addition to many of the traditional shopping venues around the city, here are a few specialty shops that might be useful on your visit.

Annam Gourmet Market – This market is an international mini-grocery store carrying Western items such as cured meats, cheese, pasta, fruit and vegetables, packaged food products, craft beer, wine, and other goods similar to what you would find in a Western gourmet market. There is a coffee lounge that serves wine and a long list of dishes including cheese boards, sandwiches, oysters, and more. In addition to the District 1 location there are two others, one each in District 2 and District 7. (**www.annam-gourmet.com**) 16-18 Hai Ba Trung (District 1) (+84 8 3822 9332)

The Warehouse Wine Store – With multiple locations in Indochina, The Warehouse imports wine from both the Old and the New World, including esteemed selections from France, Italy, Spain, California, South America and Australia. There are two locations in Ho Chi Minh City, and a few more throughout Vietnam. (**www.warehouse-asia.com**) 15/5 Le Thanh Ton (District 1) (+84 8 3824 6629)

Fahasa Bookshop – This shop provides an assorted selection of English books, international newspapers, maps, and postcards. (**www.fahasasg.com.vn**) 40 Nguyen Hue (District 1) (+84 8 3822 5446)

Massage

Finding refuge in the sanctuary in Ho Chi Minh City's many wonderful massage parlors is highly recommended, if not an absolute must. A relaxing session can be a great antidote for the frayed nerves that can develop from the din of street noise, the frightful exercise of trying to cross the street, and the many other stressful moments you are likely to endure while visiting the city. Losing yourself in the tranquility of a relaxing spa underneath gentle hands might cure whatever ails you.

While many spas in town are professional and therapeutic like those listed below, there are also several offering more illicit services. Inspecting an unfamiliar spa, including ensuring cleanliness, should provide enough clues to tell the difference. Check out online reviews as well.

Most of the major hotels offer massages. Primarily, they are two to three times more expensive than the independent parlors, but the therapists tend to be more skilled, the rooms more alluring, the atmosphere more tranquil, and there usually is (but not always) noticeably less disruptive street noise.

Here are some independent establishments to consider (appointments recommended):

Indochine – Not far from Ben Thanh Market, street noise is minimal at this location but still can be heard. Relaxing music helps to drown out some of the incessant outside horn honking. The air-conditioned rooms keep things cool during a therapeutic massage, waxing, or nail work. There are lockers underneath the massage bed. *10:00 – 22:00, daily* (**www.indochine-spa.com.vn**) 69 Thu Khoa Huan (District 1) (+84 8 3827 7188)

Temple Leaf Spa – In an appealing location near the Old Opium Refinery across from the Park Hyatt is the in-vogue Temple Leaf Spa offering body massage and comprehensive healing packages, where employees have attended the Temple Leaf Massage School for their certification in the therapeutic arts. *10:00 – 23:30, daily* (**www.templeleafspa.com**) 74 Hai Ba Trung (District 1) (+84 12 1833 2530)

Massage Enjoy – Also in a convenient location not far from Temple Leaf, Massage Enjoy is probably the most inexpensive option, yet sessions are still professional and with solid technique. You may hear street noise during your visit. The massage "rooms" are separated by curtains, meaning you might hear some grunting and yelping (and sadly, snoring) from the other massage beds. *10:00 – 22:00, daily* (**www.massageenjoy.com**) 15B3 Le Thanh Ton (District 1) (+84 8 2210 4990)

Glow Spa – This cozy spa is located close to the downtown Sheraton on Nguyen Hue Boulevard. It is another wonderfully relaxing option offering body massage and hair and nail packages. It is a mostly quiet refuge in the heart of Ho Chi Minh City. *11:00 – 22:30, daily* (**www.glowsaigon.com**) 129a Nguyen Hue (District 1) (+84 8 3823 8368)

Golden Lotus – Another spa for those on a tighter budget, this Korean-style spa is charmingly decorated, the staff is professional, and the post-massage cup of tea is a soothing perk. It is located near the strip of massage parlors adjacent to Le Than Ton Street. *09:00 – 23:00, daily* (**www.hoangsen.com**) 15 Thai Van Lung (District 1) (+84 8 3822 1515)

Miu Miu Spa – With four locations in District 1, these professionally run establishments provide convenient online booking and a full menu of unique, stress-releasing options, including Thai, Shiatsu, aroma-therapy, and ginger massage. *09:30 – 23:30, daily* (**www.miumiuspa.com**) 4 Chu Manh Trinh Street + three other locations (District 1) (+84 8 6659 3609)

Economy

Historically, agriculture has been the foundation of Vietnam's commerce and existence. Its two river deltas, long coastline, and the climatic diversity of its mountainous regions have contributed mightily to the emergence and sustainability of its many civilizations over the centuries. Even today, major industries are agricultural in nature, including the exportation of coffee, tea, rice, rubber, fruit, vegetables, and textile raw materials such as cotton.

The conflicts of the 20th century decimated much of the country's agricultural land, resulting in severe long-term effects on its economy. During the Vietnam War, millions of acres of forest and farmland were destroyed by bombs, the use of herbicides, and other kinds of chemical warfare. A heavy toll was exacted on trees, crop fields, rice paddies, and natural irrigation systems. Widespread defoliation and arable land destruction has recovered some since the conflict, but its total economic damage is difficult to calculate.

After the Vietnam War ended, the communist government adopted a centrally planned economy for the reunified nation under Soviet state-run models. This approach was largely unsuccessful and resulted in another critical blow to the nation's reeling economy. At the time, Vietnam was still one of the poorest countries in the world. A series of reforms known as *Doi Moi* ("change") were soon passed. These laws put in place the foundation for a socialist market-oriented economy that has now enabled Vietnam to move towards long-term prosperity.

In 2007, Vietnam's entry in the World Trade Organization (WTO) helped to promote market competition and increase its level of international trade. This also further accelerated Vietnam's shift towards a market economy, with less reliance on state-owned enterprises.

In 2016, the GDP (Gross Domestic Product) surpassed the $200 billion USD level. This represents nearly 7% growth from 2015. This is similar to the growth rate Vietnam experienced in 2014, so the economic prognosis continues to be favorable, placing Vietnam at #35 in the world in total GDP rankings and in the top 20 for GDP growth. With a population of ninety million, including a labor force of fifty-five million, Vietnam is still ranked #127 in the world on a GDP per capita basis, so there is still significant room for continued improvement.

The nation's economy is clearly on the upswing and is one of the fastest growing in the developing world. Agriculture now represents only 17% of the nation's GDP rather than being the dominant sector it once was. Heavy industry such as oil, steel, mining, tires, and cement, along with food processing plants and manufacturing sectors such as mobile phones, glass products, and apparel account for nearly 39% of the GDP. Services, including banking, healthcare, telecommunications, and tourism constitute nearly 44% of the GDP. Still, 40% of contributing businesses to the GDP remain state-owned in Vietnam.

Ho Chi Minh City is Vietnam's largest metropolitan economy, significantly larger than that of Hanoi. It is the heart of economic activity in Vietnam. You can sense the entrepreneurial spirit when visiting the city, with daily activity starting in the early hours, even before dawn, lasting well into the darkness of evening. Although its eight million people represent less than 10% of Vietnam's population, they contribute more than 20% of Vietnam's GDP.

The city's vibrant business culture is much more international and cosmopolitan as compared with other Vietnamese cities. International financial partnerships have been increasing. Multinational corporations such as Intel, Samsung, Microsoft, IBM, Nike, and Mercedes-Benz have all made significant investments and have hired large numbers of workers in or near the city.

The "startup" industry is booming as well. IDG Ventures Vietnam, an offshoot of IDG Ventures in the United States, has $100 million USD under management with over forty portfolio companies in Vietnam. Many of these companies have their headquarters in Ho Chi Minh City. There are significant investments in a local software park and a high-tech corridor to encourage the growth of these companies. The Ho Chi Minh City Stock Market (HOSE) currently has over three hundred listed companies.

There are also significant infrastructure investments being made. The city is currently developing an underground metro system.

The first line is expected to be completed and operational by 2020. A new international airport, which will increase air passenger capacity by 500%, is expected to be completed in 2025. Compared with many other metropolitan areas in Southeast Asia, Ho Chi Minh City has some of the faster and more reliable Internet and communications network infrastructure you will find.

Unprecedented economic progress is being made in Ho Chi Minh City. All indicators are pointing towards an extraordinarily bright, booming future for its citizens.

Film, Literature, Music

There are many exciting films and literature about Ho Chi Minh City, the former Saigon, and Vietnam as a whole. Watching or reading a few of these prior to or during your visit would be educational and likely enliven your travel experience. The music scene in Ho Chi Minh City and the rest of Vietnam is also rich with variety and talent. Here are some especially relevant, enjoyable, and thought-provoking selections:

Movies

Indochine is a 1992 film starring Catherine Deneuve (nominated for an Academy Award) set in colonial Saigon from the 1930s to the 1950s during the rise of Vietnamese nationalism.

The Quiet American is the remake of the Graham Greene film adaption from the love rivalry novel of the same name. It is set in 1952 prior to the escalation of the Vietnam War and stars Michael Caine and Brendan Fraser.

Born on the Fourth of July is Oliver Stone's adaptation of Vietnam veteran Ron Kovic's autobiography of his experiences before, during, and after the war with Tom Cruise in the leading role. Oliver Stone also directed two other films about the Vietnam War, *Platoon* and *Heaven & Earth*.

Francis Ford Coppola's 1979 *Apocalypse Now* starring Marlon Brando, Robert Duvall and Martin Sheen, is the timeless classic about the Vietnam War, nominated for Best Picture at the Academy Awards.

Documentaries

The Last Days in Vietnam is a 2014 documentary about the evacuation of Saigon in 1975. It was nominated for an Academy Award in its category.

Vietnam: A Television History is an eleven-hour DVD series created in 1983 that goes in depth to the causes, actions, and repercussions of the Vietnam War with excellent wartime footage.

The History Channel's six-episode *Vietnam in HD* released in 2011 is another in-depth look at US involvement in the war.

In 2017, PBS released its ten-episode, eighteen-hour marathon documentary entitled *The Vietnam War*, which includes interviews from more than one hundred witnesses of the conflict from multiple perspectives, including several North and South Vietnamese soldiers.

Fiction

Graham Greene's *The Quiet American* is the 1950s classic that is set in colonial Saigon from which the film of the same name is made.

Anthony Grey's celebrated *Saigon* is also an excellent choice prior to or during your trip.

Non-fiction

Nghia M. Vo's *Saigon: A History* reaches back in time and tells the story of Ho Chi Minh City from its beginnings.

William J. Duiker's *Ho Chi Minh: A Life* is a comprehensive biography of the North Vietnamese leader.

Robert McNamara's *In Retrospect* provides the former Secretary of Defense's perspective on US involvement during the escalation of the Vietnam War.

Richard Nixon's *No More Vietnams* provides the former President's views on the Vietnam War and its consequences.

Stanley Karnow's *Vietnam: A History* is considered one of the more comprehensive works on the Vietnam War, and is the basis for the aforementioned *Vietnam: A Television History*.

Music

There are many well-known musicians in Vietnam spanning many generations. From early Vietnamese traditional music, through the songs of a tumultuous 20th century, and to today's pop stars (and even a smattering of rock-n-roll and heavy metal), the music scene in Vietnam is a rich and vibrant one.

The following is a sampling of several locally revered musicians. Most of these have music that can be found on YouTube and other Internet sources if you would like to give any of them a listen, or perhaps even play as background music in your hotel room to help set the mood for your visit. You might even have the good fortune to see one or more of these musicians perform live during your visit (except those that are deceased of course). Primarily these musicians are listed because of their popularity in Ho Chi Minh City, and to provide an introduction and foundation to local music should you want to explore further.

Trinh Cong Son was a musician and composer born in 1939 to which the Trinh Restaurant (see *Where to Eat*) is dedicated. Many of his songs were of love and anti-war themes. Several were banned by the government of South Vietnam and later by the Socialist Republic of Vietnam.

Many of the songs written by Trinh Cong Son were sung by Khanh Ly (born in 1945). She began appearing professionally in Saigon clubs at the age of 17. She now lives in California.

Pham Duy, born in 1921, is known as perhaps Vietnam's most famous songwriter and has composed over one thousand songs. His music was restricted in Vietnam from 1975 to 2005. He passed away in Ho Chi Minh City in 2013.

Dam Vinh Hung, born in 1971, is a former hairdresser-turned-modern-male-pop-star in Vietnam, although his visits to the United States have been politically controversial with former South Vietnamese because of his past political affiliations.

My Tam, born in 1981 and originally from Danang, has an astonishingly powerful voice. She has recently been a judge on *Vietnam Idol*.

Ho Ngoc Ha, born in 1984 in Hanoi, got her start winning first prize in a Vietnamese supermodel contest. She is known for a catchy, bold, sexy performing style with creative dance moves and a high sense of fashion. She now resides in Ho Chi Minh City.

Born in 1987, Le Cat Trong Ly has become known for her modern brand of Vietnamese folk music.

Miu Le, born in Ho Chi Minh City in 1991, is a more recent popular vocalist, especially in vogue with the youth. In addition to her singing career she is also a popular actor.

Side Trips

Ho Chi Minh City and all it has to offer is a great excursion on its own. Still, most visitors will also look to travel to additional places in Vietnam for an even greater number of cultural experiences and to add dimension to their trip. Here are some ideas for side trips near Ho Chi Minh City (and some not so near) for added variety and completeness of an itinerary.

Hue

The Imperial City of Hue (pronounced "hway") is a one-hour flight from Ho Chi Minh City and worth a visit for its renowned cuisine and profound history.

Between 1802 and 1945, this city was the capital of the Nguyen dynasty and the Nguyen lords who gained control of all of Vietnam until Emperor Bao Dai abdicated the throne in 1945. The Imperial City of Hue, somewhat comparable to the Forbidden City in Beijing, China as an emperor's stronghold, is full of UNESCO World Heritage sites. For a long time, many of these old imperial sites were not viewed favorably by the communist regime and historic buildings were neglected. Now, for the sake of tourism, many of these old sites are being restored, including the tombs of various emperors.

During the Vietnam War, the city was the location of the Battle of Hue in 1968 as part of the Tet Offensive and much of it was destroyed. While not a military victory, it was a major psychological turning point for the communists. Stanley Kubrick's film *Full Metal Jacket* portrayed the Battle of Hue. Mark Bowden's new book released in 2017, *Hue 1968: A Turning Point of the American War in Vietnam*, also focuses on the Battle of Hue.

Today, the city is also famous for its *thuc an Hue* cuisine, known in Ho Chi Minh City as "Hue food" when translated. Its imperial cuisine, a historical and creative form of royal Vietnamese "tapas," along with its famous traditional spicier food can be discovered here in Hue. Now, many of the classic dishes, such as *bun bo Hue*, *chao gio*, and *chao tom*, can also be found in Ho Chi Minh City. In addition, there is a plentiful amount of vegetarian cuisine available in Hue because of the extensive Buddhist culture that exists. See *Cuisine of Ho Chi Minh City* for more detail.

The best way to get to Hue is by commercial airlines from Ho Chi Minh City. The cities of Danang and Hoi An are nearby, reachable by private driver in two hours or so.

Hoi An

Just south of Danang is the ancient Cham spice-trading port town of Hoi An. The UNESCO World Heritage site is a charming, well-preserved riverside town only a few miles from the ocean. A key commercial center through the 19th century, the silting of the river left the town in commercial decline until the 1990s when a tourism boom emerged, transforming it into a charming riverside tourist town.

The delightful pedestrian maze of streets features an ancient city set among the canals and bridges that is ideal for strolling. There is a beautiful Japanese covered bridge and pagoda set on the river. There are significant Asian and European influences throughout the town, signifying its long trading history. A by-the-river local-cuisine dinner among the glowing silk lanterns in the evening is a definite highlight. The city is also famous for its on-demand fitted suit tailoring. Be sure to visit the nearby beach on the South China Sea, a preferred choice by many for accommodations.

The ancient Champa village of My Son with its relic Hindu temples is nearby. A commercial flight into Danang and then hiring a driver is the best way to travel to Hoi An.

Mui Ne

Originally a backpacker's destination known for its beautiful red, orange, and white sand dunes, Mui Ne is a peaceful, seaside resort town in hired-driver distance from Ho Chi Minh City. You will find fishing boats, a seductive assortment of local seafood, a growing number of resorts, and on-the-beach bungalows underneath groves of coconut trees (be wary of the thud of falling coconuts on your roof in the late moonlight).

The city is near urban Phan Thiet (reachable by train) and is a surfing destination from August through December when the heavy rains occur northward along the coast.

Vung Tau

Vung Tau, meaning "anchorage," is a beachside hotel and resort town once visited by European trading ships. Known as Cap St. Jacques during French colonization, it has a landmark governor's mansion from the period. At the time, large sailing vessels brought visitors and future residents through here on their way up the Saigon River to reach their destination of Saigon. It is still a winding four-hour journey upriver (mostly because it is difficult to navigate) for larger vessels.

During the Vietnam War, the island was used for R&R purposes by the American military. It also became a major departure point after the Fall of Saigon where Vietnamese boat people fleeing the country launched their rafts as they headed eastward to escape the encroaching communists.

Today, along with several beachside hotels, there are many pagodas and temples to visit in the city. There are also many resorts scheduled for construction over the next several years. Except for a handful of existing holiday retreats, many of the current accommodations are meager and the public beaches themselves are not quite world-class. Still, a day trip or a night or two can be rewarding, as the seafood here can be exceptional. As the resort selection continues to develop and increase, the city and beach will hopefully only improve.

You can hire a personal driver to take you to Vung Tau or take the older Russian-built hydrofoil boats that leave from the end of Dong Khoi Street for a ninety-minute journey. It is possible due to past mechanical issues that this service might be discontinued, however a company called Vina Express has operated them recently. As of late the service has been off and on. Check **vinaexpress.com.vn** for current information. Vung Tau Airport (VTG) is also served by commercial airlines.

Coastal city of Vung Tau

Grand Ho Tram Strip

The Grand Ho Tram Strip is approximately forty kilometers up the coast from Vung Tau. Its primary attraction is the large, ocean-adjacent casino resort and complex, the Grand Ho Tram Resort (**www.thegrandhotram.com**). You can take a bus from either the Vung Tau ferry terminal (forty-five minutes) or from District 1 in Ho Chi Minh City (two hours) in a Wi-Fi-enabled coach, available a few times per day (see the website for more information). You can also hire a private car to get here.

The oceanfront resort has over eleven hundred rooms, the casino (slot machines and gaming tables), a Greg Norman-designed golf course, multiple pools, a nightclub, a two-kilometer-long beach, and several dining options including Chinese, Western, and Vietnamese.

Phu Quoc

Phu Quoc, Vietnam's largest island, provides beaches, snorkeling, some of the best seafood in Vietnam, and plenty of additional island sights. The island, situated in the Gulf of Thailand west of the mainland and just off the southern Cambodian coast, was used by the South Vietnamese as a prison during the Vietnam War. It held as many as 40,000 Viet Cong prisoners. The infamous "coconut prison" can be toured today.

The island only became part of Vietnam in 1949 when it was granted to the Vietnamese by the French. This is still somewhat in dispute today by Cambodia, and likely part of the reason the northern section of the island is a Vietnamese military base. The island was especially at issue in the late 1970s during the Vietnam-Cambodian War.

The island is famous for its fish sauce manufacturing, black pepper, and more recently its pearl farming. There are many tours available that provide insight to the diversity of the island.

Long Beach provides many different types of accommodation, including resorts and beachside bungalows for those who want to hear the waves throughout the night, sleeping underneath the coconut trees and the shimmering constellations.

To get to Phu Quoc island from Ho Chi Minh City, there are direct flights available to Phu Quoc's international airport available from Vietnam Airlines and a couple of other regional airlines. There are also bus-plus-boat passes available from Ho Chi Minh City for budget-minded travelers.

In an effort to encourage tourism, a travel visa is not required to visit the island of Phu Quoc, unlike mainland Vietnam. Visa-free stays of up to thirty days are allowed.

Bai Sao Beach, Phu Quoc Island

Dalat

Dalat is a charming mountain town in the central highlands known for its lakes, waterfalls, gardens and cool weather. Its temperate climate, mainly in the 60s Fahrenheit (16-18 Celsius) most of the year, inspired the French colonials to build a retreat here to escape the tropical heat of the cities. Used as a honeymoon location by young Vietnamese newlyweds, Dalat has streets lined with old French villas and an Alpine feel, which of course was the original intention. In its early days, it served as an exotic hunting location. It was the summer capital of French Indochina during the Second World War, and the emperor Bao Dai had his summer palace here that can be visited today.

There are indigenous ethnic tribes living nearby that sell their crafts and various agricultural goods at local markets, including cherries, strawberries, cauliflower, avocados, and more, many of which are unique to the Dalat region and its climate in Vietnam. Dalat is also famous for its various types of rice cakes, including "Dalat

Pizza," an egg and rice-baked pancake dish. Jams made from the local produce harvest are available throughout the town.

The rainy season, from April to November, can indeed bring afternoon showers, but the myriad, quaint coffee shops around town will keep you warm. Dalat is in the central highlands after all, the heart of Vietnam's coffee bean growing fields.

You can travel to Dalat from Ho Chi Minh City by car and driver, but the 180-mile trip can take six hours. Vietnam Airlines provides fifty-minute flights to Dalat Airport (DLI). There are many resorts to stay at both in and around Dalat, some grand, and some adequate for the budget-conscious. You can even play a round of golf in Dalat.

Nha Trang

Beautiful waterfront Nha Trang is famous for its lobster and fresh seafood cuisine. The active fishing community provides its bounty. With its green coastal mountains (or perhaps large hills) and blue waters, this seaside beach town, speckled with former remains of the Champa civilization (such as the Po Nagar Towers), is reminiscent of Hawaii.

Known for its beautiful bay, its energetic nightlife, diverse restaurants, its many beach resorts (some quite luxurious), and its scuba diving, it is a stop for several Southeast Asian cruise ships and at times can be heavily touristy. The Vin Pearl Resort, the Diamond Bay Resort (where a recent Miss Universe pageant was held), and the Ana Mandara Resort are three of the most famous (and pricey) beach resorts in Vietnam. They can provide some tranquility away from the well-populated local beaches. There are many more cost-conscious hotel options, especially along the manicured shorefront. There are several hiking trails and coastal islands to explore, including the touristy "monkey island."

Historically, nearby Cam Ranh Bay served as an important naval base for the US during the Vietnam War (and later the Soviets).

Cam Ranh Airport is where all commercial air traffic, both international and domestic, services Nha Trang.

Flying is the best option from Ho Chi Minh City. If you combine Nha Trang with either Mui Ne or Dalat, hiring a private driver for the entire trip is another option.

Mekong Delta

The Mekong Delta, commonly called the "rice bowl" of Vietnam, is a maze of rivers, canals, mangrove forests, sampan boats, floating villages, and water markets. It comprises the land around where the Mekong River empties out of Vietnam and into the sea.

The Mekong River, approximately 2700 miles long, has its source in the Tibetan Plateau of China. It then winds through Myanmar, Laos, Thailand, and Cambodia before passing west of Ho Chi Minh City, through its delta region, and into the Gulf of Thailand near Phu Quoc. It is one of the most biologically diverse regions in the world, with thousands of unique species of animals and plants, and new ones discovered all the time.

The Mekong Delta region is known for its abundance of vegetables and tropical fruit, including coconuts, limes, mangoes, dragon fruit, lychees, and papaya. These diverse jungle flavors are a major part of its cuisine, along with freshwater fish, including many rice- and rice paper-based dishes. Its fresh produce, herbs, and spices are the pillars of southern Vietnamese cuisine.

Touring the Mekong River on a boat with one of the several tour companies is a side trip highlight of any visit to Ho Chi Minh City. One can visit the floating and riverside traditional villages, watch handmade coconut candy produced, gawk at water buffalo, float down side canals, and see the village-based manufacturing of rice paper, all enjoyed around local cuisine and the friendly company of the Mekong Delta inhabitants. Exo Travel, Ann Tours, and the government-run Saigon Tourist are options for Mekong River excursions. There are day trips from Ho Chi Minh City, or you can also stay overnight in Can Tho, the largest city in the Mekong Delta, and visit its colorful floating market, see its old port, stay in a modern resort, and sample its classic dishes in various local eateries.

You can also pass through the Mekong Delta en route to Phu Quoc.

Hanoi

If you have the time, Hanoi is a great addition to your Ho Chi Minh City itinerary. The city's proximity to the Red River makes for a temperate climate. You can experience the four seasons and enjoy a respite from the intense heat of Ho Chi Minh City. There is also a great deal of cultural, historical, and gastronomical highlights to experience. With many daily non-stop flights to Hanoi from Ho Chi Minh City, it is an essential base for visits to travelers' favorites such as Halong Bay, Sapa, and Ninh Binh. Noi Bai International Airport (HAN) is the largest in Vietnam with its new international terminal completed in 2015.

Hanoi, established as a settlement over one thousand years ago and therefore much older than Ho Chi Minh City, was the political capital of Vietnam from 1010 to 1802, and then the capital of French Indochina from 1902 to 1954 (Hue was the imperial capital of the Vietnamese Nguyen dynasty from 1802 to 1945). It was the capital of North Vietnam from 1954 to 1976. From 1976 until today it is the capital of a unified Vietnam. There are many related political sights to see such as the Presidential Palace and the mausoleum of Ho Chi Minh.

The oldest university in Vietnam, St. Joseph's Cathedral, the venerable Metropole Hotel of Somerset Maugham and Graham Greene fame, and a seemingly endless labyrinth of charming tree-lined streets, colonial architecture, shops, and eateries constitute the Old Quarter of Hanoi. It has been dubbed by some as the Paris of the Orient. The pleasant Hoan Kiem Lake with its ancient walking bridge and pagodas serves as the Old Quarter's center and is near many quaint Old Quarter hotels.

From a traditional dining standpoint, it is an excellent opportunity to experience northern Vietnamese cuisine, including the birthplace of *pho* and Hanoi's unique take on the dish. You will also find *cha ca* (dill and catfish in a clay pot), *nem* (thick, deep fried spring rolls), and *bun cha Hanoi* (Hanoi's version of grilled pork meatballs and vermicelli noodles). There is a long list of beautiful, upscale northern Vietnamese restaurants to rival the offerings of Ho Chi Minh City.

Modern Hanoi is surging with many new skyscrapers and international hotels popping up frequently, especially around the West Lake area, which also is a home to an increasing number of expats. The city represents a tremendous opportunity to experience the Vietnam of past and present.

Hoan Kiem Lake in Hanoi at night

Halong Bay

Halong Bay, a UNESCO world heritage site since 1994, requires considerable effort to visit from Ho Chi Minh City. The bay is in the Gulf of Tonkin. First, you must fly to Hanoi, probably stay at least the night, and then arrange an organized tour with a three-to-four-hour van ride to Halong Bay if you have not already booked it in advance in Ho Chi Minh City. You will then board your *junk*, a replica of an ancient sailing ship, typically for a noon-to-noon (or longer) overnight excursion.

Though the journey will be long, it is well worth the trip and effort. Acknowledged by many as the top tourist destination in all of Vietnam, Halong Bay is a spectacular seascape consisting of over sixteen hundred monolithic, pillar-like limestone rock formation islands. *Ha long* means "descending dragon" in Vietnamese. Legend has it that this bay was the realm of ancient flying dragons that protected the Vietnamese coast from invaders. On most tours, you will visit floating fishing villages, caves, grottos, a beach or two, a famous pagoda, and see the various rock formations that have been weathered away by the elements over the millennia creating their unique shapes.

If time permits, a visit to Halong Bay is an exhilarating and breathtaking addition to any trip to Ho Chi Minh City.

About the Author

Robert J. Brauer travels frequently to Vietnam and is focused on interests such as Vietnamese history, culture, local gastronomy, and all things Ho Chi Minh City. He has traveled extensively not only within Vietnam but also around the globe, including much of Asia, Europe, North America, South America, and Australia. Born in Ohio, he now resides in California. Robert can be contacted at robert@travelgalley.com.

Index